Praxis Core Study Guide 2021-2022

468 Test Questions and Detailed Answer Explanations for the Reading, Writing and Math Sections 5713, 5723, 5733 (Includes 3 Full-Length Practice Exams)

Table of Contents

Background

Universities and colleges use the Praxis Core test to evaluate prospective students enrolled in United States teacher education programs. The test is designed to be taken early in an individual's college career.

In some states, the Praxis Core test is one of the requirements for eligibility for obtaining teacher licensing, making it mandatory for individuals who desire a teaching career.

The Educational Testing Service (ETS) created the Praxis Core examination to ensure that only qualified teachers staff the education sector. The test meets the Common Core State Standards (CCSS) and the College and Career Readiness Standards (CCR).

The test will assess your skills in mathematics, reading and writing. There are 56 multiple-choice questions in the reading section that cover some key ideas, such as language skills, structure, ideas and knowledge integration. You are expected to complete this section in 85 minutes.

In the writing section, you will answer 40 multiple-choice questions and questions about two essays. These will cover text purpose, text type, writing research skills and language. In all, you have 100 minutes to complete the writing section.

In the math section, you have 85 minutes to answer 56 multiple-choice questions that will test your knowledge of algebra and functions, numbers and quantities, statistics and probability and geometry. Do not worry about bringing a calculator to the exam center; you will be provided with an on-screen one.

Test Format

The Praxis Core is a computer-based examination conducted in English. The multiple-choice questions are taken from three major areas: reading, writing and math.

Candidates who speak English as a second language may apply for 50 percent additional testing time. However, note that the additional time does not apply to language tests. Furthermore, you cannot change your test center or tests after completing your registration. Visit the ETS website to learn the specific requirements to be granted testing accommodations.

How to Prepare for the Test

Your preparation for the examination will determine your performance to a great extent. To increase your chances of passing, you must first learn about the structure and general content of the exam. Then, prepare a plan of study.

Use good material to prepare for the exam, such as this study guide. Go through it as many times as necessary. The more you study the material, the better you will do. Use the Question and Answer sections to your advantage. Practice, practice, practice.

Taking the Test

You have 270 minutes to complete the test, which is conducted all year round. You can register for and take the test at your convenience. ETS has Prometric Testing Centers around the country. Visit any of the centers in your neighborhood for registration and to pick a date for the test. If you cannot find any testing centers near you, contact the examination body for assistance.

How to Register for the Exam

You can register for the examination online with either your credit/debit or via PayPal.

Once you are done with the registration, print your admission slip and keep it safe. This ticket is very important because it contains your reporting time and test center address.

Have a hard copy of the exam ticket with you when you go to the center. Although it is not mandatory, test center personnel may request the ticket, and they may not accept an electronic copy of the ticket on your phone.

You can also register via your cell phone. To use this method, you must create a Praxis account online. Then call ETS at 1-800-772-9476 between 8 a.m. and 6 p.m. eastern time, Monday through Friday. You will be able to pay over the phone via a credit/debit card. Note that phone registration costs an additional $35.

You are required to contact ETS a couple of days before your test date to confirm your registration.

Test Costs

The Praxis Core test costs $190. If you register by phone, you will pay an additional $35, for a total of $225.

Where to Take the Test

You can select the most convenient test center from some universities, Prometric Testing Centers and other approved locations across the United States. ETS also allows candidates who meet special requirements to take the examination from home.

Note that the home examination is identical in format and content to regular tests given in test centers. The home test is conducted every day of the week between 10 a.m. and 1 p.m. for qualified candidates.

Check the ETS website to determine your eligibility.

How to Retake the Test

You are allowed to retake the examination 35 days after the initial examination. The same rule applies if you cancel your previous test scores for whatever reason.

However, if you violate this restriction and attempt to take the test earlier, your initial test result will be canceled and you will forfeit the examination fee. No refunds are available under these circumstances.

What To Do

Be punctual on the examination day.

Take a government-issued ID, such as a passport or a driver's license, to the exam location. The examiners will identify you through your ID, so the attached photo must be clear. It must also show your signature and full name for easy identification.

You are not allowed to leave the test center while the test is ongoing. You also cannot leave your assigned seat while taking the test.

Do not take any electronic device into the test room. Watches, phones, cameras and other devices should be kept in the assigned locker for safekeeping. If these devices are found on you, you will be penalized.

The examiners will provide you with pen and paper. Do not bring your own. If you take them with you to the testing center, place them in the locker with your other personal belongings.

What Not To Do

Do not go into the test center with objects such as calculators, pagers, phones, test aids, etc. If you are caught with one, you run the risk of being barred from taking the test.

No talking is allowed during the examination. You can communicate with the examiner only when necessary. Violators of this rule may lose their right to take the examination.

How to Interpret Your Score

When you are finished with the test, you will be given the option to either cancel or report your score. If you choose to report your score, you cannot cancel it again. If you decide to cancel your score, it will not be reported and you will not get a refund.

During registration you are allowed to choose up to four licensing agencies or institutions that can receive your score on your behalf. The teacher credentialing agency in some states, such as South Dakota, Oregon, California and others, will receive a copy of your scores. You can check the ETS website for a complete list of these states or territories.

Your score result will tell you whether you passed the test or not. It will also provide raw points in each category, give a range of possible scores and state your highest score if you previously took the test within the last decade.

State Requirements

Check with your state for any state-specific requirements before you proceed with the examination. Each state also decides how it defines a passing score. So if you do not pass in your state, you can check other states to see if you pass there.

Praxis Core Exam Tips

The following preparation tips can help you prepare for the test.

1. Do not cram. Cramming is counterproductive as it increases your chances of forgetting everything you learn before the examination. Rather, study a little bit each day. That will boost your memorization skills and enable you to perform well.
2. Make sure you know how to get to the exam location ahead of time. Visit the test center several days before the exam and take note of traffic conditions, routes, parking spaces and other important information so you're not late.
3. Get sufficient rest before the examination day.
4. Stay hydrated before the examination. And do not go into the test hungry.
5. Try to answer all the questions. You will not be penalized for wrong answers, but you will earn no points for a skipped question. If you come across difficult questions, try to narrow your answer down to one or two options, then make your best guess.
6. If you have some time to spare after completing the test, use that time to review the questions and your answers.
7. Prioritize your studying. You will be tested in writing, reading and mathematics. Focus on areas where you are less skilled and spend less time studying the areas where you are strong.
8. Make time to familiarize yourself with the examination. Learn the general structure of the test. This includes the timing, layout, scoring and other relevant areas that will improve your performance.

Chapter One: Reading

Your reading and comprehension ability will be assessed in this section of the test. This includes your ability to make inferences, draw logical conclusions from reading materials, understand figures of speech and idiomatic expressions and use other skills that enhance your ability to read a passage and understand the context.

The reading test is divided into three parts. The first part is the Key Ideas and Details section, where your understanding of a passage's content will be tested. You are also required to understand what the content of a passage implies. This may call on your ability to make inferences, understand figures of speech and use the context of a word or an expression to deduce the meaning of an unfamiliar word. You must be able to identify the main ideas in a paragraph or a sentence and comprehensively understand the entire passage.

The second section is Craft, Structure and Language Skills. The section focuses on your understanding of the way an author organizes information, uses words and employs writing techniques to communicate a particular meaning.

Lastly, there is the Integration of Knowledge and Ideas section. Here you are expected to draw inferences from a passage by pulling together necessary pieces of information from multiple ideas to arrive at a logical conclusion.

Key Ideas and Details

Figures of Speech

A figure of speech is a phrase or word that has a meaning that is different from its literal meaning. Here are some common figures of speech you may come across in a passage.

Simile

A simile is a figure of speech that is used for comparing two things that are not alike. Similes often utilize the words *as* or *like*. A simile compares two unrelated things.

Some common examples of similes are:

- He is as cool as a cucumber.
- His smile is as bright as the sun.
- She is as thin as a needle.
- It is tough as nails.
- Her heart was beating like a drum.
- She walks like a goddess.

Similes make language more descriptive and creative.

For instance, the expression "He is as tall as a mountain" does not literally mean that the subject's height is on the same level as that of a mountain. However, it creates the impression of someone who is extraordinarily tall.

Hyperbole

Hyperbole refers to using exaggeration as a figure of speech. It is commonly referred to as *exaggeration*, *amplification* or *overstatement*. Such exaggeration shows emphasis or drives home an important point.

Examples of hyperbole include:

- I am so hungry that I could eat a whole elephant.
- She has cleaned her room a million times today.
- The weather was so cold that polar bears were wearing jackets and hats.
- He is so powerful that he can move a mountain.

Alliteration

Alliteration is the repetition of the initial consonant sounds in neighboring syllables or words, even if they have different spellings. It is also known as *initial rhyme*, *head rhyme*, *reiteration* or *iteration*.

Examples of alliteration include:

- Peter Piper picked a peck of pickled peppers.
- A black bug bit a big black bear.
- She sells seashells by the seashore.

Metaphor

Although there is a similarity between a simile and a metaphor, a simile makes a comparison with words such as *like* and *as*, but a metaphor uses direct comparison without these connector words.

Properly used, metaphors help create a lasting impression and leave a strong image in the mind of an audience.

Examples of metaphors include:

- She is drowning in an ocean of grief.
- You broke her heart.
- There is a ray of hope on the horizon.

- This is the icing on the cake.
- He is the black sheep of the family.

Personification

Personification refers to the attribution of human characteristics to inanimate things.

Examples of personification include:

- The sunlight dances carelessly on her skin.
- These plants are begging for water.
- I woke up to the yelling of the alarm clock.
- She heard the thunder grumbling ceaselessly.

Paradox

A paradox is a self-contradictory statement. A paradox is simultaneously true and untrue. Paradoxical statements are apparently valid reasoning, but on proper scrutiny may lead to a contradictory conclusion.

Paradoxes help writers depict the reality of life. We live in a world that is full of contradiction, and this explains why some people have seemingly contradictory personalities and behaviors.

Some examples of paradoxical statements are:

- Standing is more tiring than walking.
- Less is more.
- You can make money by spending it.
- This is the beginning of the end.

Onomatopoeia

Onomatopoeia refers to a word that resembles the sound described by the word. Examples of onomatopoeia include:

- The heavy bag fell into the water with a huge splash.
- He fell on the canvas with a thump.
- The ball whirred past him.

Pun

A pun is a form of wordplay, with the primary objective of achieving a rhetorical or humorous effect. Puns are otherwise known as *paronomasia*. They are based on words that have similar sounds, spellings or meaning, such as homonyms, homophones or homographs.

Some examples of puns include:

- The two pianists are always in a chord.
- I have been to my dentist several times, and I know the drill.
- You should trust the glue salesman because he sticks to his word.
- The library is the tallest building in the town because it has hundreds of stories.

Synecdoche

This is a figure of speech in which part of something is used to represent the whole, or the whole represents the part.

Some examples of synecdoche include:

- Check out my new wheels.
- I just got myself a nice place to crash.
- The police are around the corner.
- We're waiting for the Pentagon's response to the allegations.

In each of the sentences above, a part is used to represent the whole. For instance, *wheels* represents a car and *Pentagon* represents the government. Some common words that are used to represent the whole include:

- *Sails* mostly refers to ships.
- *Boots* are the synecdoche for *soldiers.*
- Eyewear is represented by *glasses.*

The following are some wholes that are used to represent the part:

- *Society*
- *World*
- *Kleenex*
- *Milk.*

Irony

Irony is a figure of speech that is used to express a sharp contrast between an expression and its meaning.

Some examples of irony include:

- The motivational speaker is depressed.

- The fire station was burned to the ground.
- The 6'10" basketball player is nicknamed *dwarf.*
- The fear of long words is called hippopotomonstrosesquippedaliophobia.

Oxymoron

In an oxymoron, two words with contradictory meanings are used together in the same sentence.

Examples of oxymorons include:

- Old news
- Small crowd
- Stupidly intelligent
- Bittersweet
- Definitely maybe
- Alone together
- Deafening silence
- Clearly confused
- Noticeably absent
- Open secret
- Virtual reality
- Random order.

Take a look at some of the examples above and see the comparison. For instance, in *old news*, *old* and *news* are antonyms. *Deafening silence* also shows two opposite words used together. How can silence, a state of muteness, be deafening?

You will come across these figures of speech and several others from time to time while reading. Understanding them and how they are used will aid your comprehension. It will also enable you to make logical inferences from study materials.

Idiomatic Expressions

Some texts may contain idiomatic expressions. Idioms are groups of words or phrases that have connotative meanings. Thus, without understanding what an idiom means, it is difficult to understand its meaning in a sentence. Here are some common examples of idioms and their meanings.

The ball is in your court: This idiom means you now have the responsibility of making the next decision or taking the next step.

Example: *This book has been designed to help you pass the Praxis Core examination. The ball is now in your court.*

Don't judge a book by its cover: Do not make a hasty judgment of someone or something based on appearance.

Example: *Although she is seemingly shorter than her friends on the basketball team, don't judge a book by its cover. She may surprise you yet.*

Cross that bridge when you come to it: Deal with a problem when and if it arises.

Example: *While I was thinking too much about how to cope with college, my mother told me that I'm still in high school and will cross that bridge when I come to it.*

In the heat of the moment: Overwhelmed by current happenings.

Example: *In the heat of the moment, he made a wrong decision that eventually had a massive negative impact on his career.*

Give someone a taste of their own medicine: Treat someone as they have treated others.

Example: *When Tony eventually stood up to the bully, he gave him a taste of his own medicine.*

Bite off more than you can chew: Attempt to do something very difficult.

Example: *The student tried to juggle school, three sports teams and a full-time job. She swiftly learned she'd bitten off more than she could chew.*

Your guess is as good as mine: I have no idea either.

Example: *When I asked him when the pandemic will be over, he simply said, "Your guess is as good as mine."*

Stir up a hornet's nest: Deliberately provoke trouble.

Example: *Asking such a sensitive question is tantamount to stirring up a hornet's nest.*

Raining cats and dogs: Rain heavily.

Example: *We couldn't keep our date with our friends yesterday because it rained cats and dogs.*

Have one's back against the wall: Be in a difficult situation with no chance of escape.

Example: *When you have your back against the wall, you can always ask friends, family, colleagues or experts for help.*

Keep someone or something at arm's length: Steer clear of them.

Example: *After hearing about my new boss' moodiness, I decided to keep him at arm's length as much as possible.*

Once in a blue moon: Rarely.

Example: *The retired farmer visits his old farm once in a blue moon.*

Burn the midnight oil: To work or study late into the night.

Example: *While preparing for his final examination, Kenny burned the midnight oil for days on end.*

Handle with kid gloves: Treat something with care and extreme tact.

Example: *Our daughter is hypersensitive and thus needed to be handled with kid gloves.*

Between the devil and the deep blue sea: Having to choose between two unpleasant alternatives.

Example: *Having to choose between missing the examination and missing the job interview is like choosing between the devil and the deep blue sea.*

As indicated in the examples above, you must understand a specific idiom before you can make sense of its meaning. You obviously cannot depend on guesses or context.

How to Identify the Main Ideas of a Text

When reading, you must understand the main ideas in the text before you can understand the text as a whole. The main idea refers to the primary concept the author wishes to communicate to an audience.

Sometimes, the main idea may be expressed directly as a topic sentence. The topic sentence helps you understand what the paragraph is about, while some supporting details may be provided in subsequent paragraphs to help develop the subject fully.

When reading multi-paragraph articles, you may find the main idea in the article's thesis statement, fully supported by some smaller points that highlight the main idea. So, how do you find the main ideas of a paragraph? The following helpful tips will enable you to do that with ease.

1. Identify the topic. This involves understanding the primary objective of the paragraph. What or whom is it about?
2. Summarize the passage after reading it thoroughly. Make it a practice to express each passage in your own words to understand it better.
3. You may gain an insight into the main idea by looking at the passage's first and last paragraphs. Most authors put the main ideas in these parts of their articles.
4. While analyzing the first and last paragraphs, pay attention to some words, such as *in contrast*, *but*, *nevertheless* and *however*. Some authors use these words to contrast the first idea, indicating that the second idea is actually the paragraph's main idea.
5. Use questions to identify the main ideas in a paragraph. When you are done with a paragraph, ask yourself what message the author is trying to get across. Does the paragraph or passage discuss a group of people, a person, or a thing? Does the information make reference to a time or a name? If something happens in the passage, can you find a plausible explanation for the occurrence? These and other related questions may help you identify the main idea in the passage or paragraph.
6. Find structural keywords. Each paragraph contains some important words that will help you find answers to questions that will help you to identify the main ideas. These are structural keywords. Some examples of key words are *however*, *but* and *although*. When you see these, be on the lookout for a contrast. Other words that may indicate the continuation of the paragraph's main idea are *and*, *as* and *moreover*. When you see such words, check the surrounding text. It will give you a clue about the main idea.

Denotative and Connotative Meanings

There are two major ways of describing words' meanings: connotative and denotative. When you look up the meaning of a new word in the dictionary, you are searching for the denotative, or literal, meaning.

Conversely, verbs, nouns, adverbs and adjectives are not limited to their basic meanings. The emotional meanings constitute their connotative meanings. Let's make the distinction between the two with some examples.

- I love my black and blue shirt.
- He was beaten black and blue.

In these two examples, *black and blue* has different meanings. In the former sentence, it refers to a combination of two colors, while in the latter, it explains the degree of a terrible beating—a different meaning entirely. While the former is denotative, the latter is connotative.

- The hotel is cheap.

Denotatively, the word *cheap* means *affordable*. Connotatively, though, it may also mean *of low quality*. Thus, when you come across a word, you may have to determine its meaning by asking whether it suggests its connotative or denotative meaning. Failure to identify this may cause you to misunderstand a paragraph.

Critical Skills for Reading and Comprehension

The following skills are crucial for reading comprehension. These skills will boost your ability to understand a text, analyze it and evaluate its content.

Critical Reading

Critical reading involves engaging meaningfully in whatever you are reading by asking relevant questions that will deepen your understanding.

When you are reading, your focus should not be only on the author's opinion. Instead, try to examine the author's message and analyze it critically, looking for information that may help you better understand the message. You should also look for oversights, limitations and arguments that may enable you to see if the content is flawed. Afterward, you may draw a reasonable conclusion that will deepen your knowledge of the subject matter.

Critical reading requires that you reflect on some important things, such as the message directed at the reader through the text. When you have read a piece critically, you should be able to paraphrase the key points in your words. If necessary, take some notes.

Use the SQ3R Reading Technique

The SQ3R is a popular, effective reading strategy that you can adapt to a wide range of reading materials and purposes. The acronym means Survey, Question, Read, Recall and Review. Let's consider each part of the technique.

Survey

While surveying a passage, scan and skim the text. The goal is to glean a general overview of the material before embarking on the actual reading.

While skimming, your focus is on the text only. This may result in lower word recognition and less understanding of the denotative meanings of some words. Skimming is best done by reading the text's introductory and concluding paragraphs. Search the material for headings and subheadings. These will give you a general insight into the material's content.

Scanning, on the other hand, refers to looking for key words and specific text. For example, when you are searching for a specific word in a dictionary, you are scanning. You use the same technique when searching for someone's phone number in a telephone directory.

Scanning requires more attention to detail and better word recognition than skimming. Although they differ significantly, skimming and scanning are two powerful tools you can use in surveying a text.

Question

Before you start reading a text, asking some questions may aid your understanding. First ask yourself the objective of the reading. Is it for entertainment? Are you reading for academic purposes? Are there other reasons why the text is important to you? When you ask these questions in advance, they will guide you through the reading process. How? Because such questions give you a reading purpose, and you will want to satisfy the purpose or find satisfying answers to your questions. This will undoubtedly increase your understanding of the text.

Questions can include "Do I have any background knowledge about the subject?" and "What message is the author trying to convey?" These are just some samples. Ask as many questions as possible to aid your understanding.

Read

While reading, have some goals in mind. Carefully consider the author's intended message. This may call on your critical thinking and analysis skills. Then, try to find answers to your questions. The more answers you find, the better your understanding of the text. If you cannot answer all the questions in the first attempt, you may have to go over the text again.

Recall

When reading, your goal is to retain as much information as you can. From time to time, try to recall the previous lessons from a text. This allows you to focus on the main points, and aids your concentration and comprehension. It also enables you to assimilate and retain the important points.

Review

Finally, review the material. Ask yourself if you fully understood the author's message. What about the main points? Have you identified them all? Are there some areas where more clarification or information is needed?

Take out your notes while reviewing the material and go through them. The little pieces of information you jotted down here and there will contribute significantly to your comprehension.

Fluency Skills

Fluency is your ability to read with accuracy, speed and proper expression. For comprehension purposes, you must be able to read fluently both silently and aloud.

To develop your fluency and, indirectly, your comprehension skills, you must understand the three components of reading fluency. These are accuracy, speed and prosody.

Speed: As a fluent reader, you must read at a rate that is appropriate for your age. This includes your ability to scan words in advance. This skill is very important when attempting time-based comprehension tests. You do not have all the time in the world to read the passage and answer the questions.

Accuracy: Accurate reading is a hallmark of a good reader. You must be able to recognize words with ease. Your accuracy should not be affected by unfamiliar words because you have the skills to find your way around such words without allowing them to break the flow of reading.

Readers with accuracy issues cannot read fluently. They are prone to making mistakes while reading and generally tend to skip words. They also struggle with word recognition and substitute one word for another, especially homophones.

There is a connection between accuracy and speed. If you can read accurately, your reading speed will automatically increase.

Prosody: The third component of reading fluency is prosody. When reading aloud, fluent readers use prosody, such as stress, pitch and timing to convey meaning.

On the other hand, dysfluent readers, rather than reading in chunks or phrases, read word by word. They don't use appropriate intonation when reading.

Note that if you exhibit the reading traits of a dysfluent reader, you are more prone to reading and comprehension issues. Your inability to read fluently will undermine your ability to read and understand.

Vocabulary Skills

Another obstacle that may stand between you and comprehension is a limited vocabulary. How can you make logical inferences from a passage if you cannot understand the majority of the text?

As you prepare for the Praxis Core examination, consider expanding your vocabulary with these tips.

Read: Reading is one of the best ways you can improve your vocabulary. Read literary works, novels, magazines, news articles and other pieces of writing that will expose you to a wide range of unfamiliar words. As you come across these new words, learn their meanings and applications. Gradually, you will add new words to your vocabulary.

Use a thesaurus and dictionary: Dictionaries and thesauruses are available in software, print or online. You can use these tools to improve your vocabulary. As you come across unfamiliar or difficult words, use these resources to learn their pronunciation, spellings, meanings, antonyms and synonyms.

Learn about word roots: Another important tool that can improve your vocabulary is to learn about words' roots, such as prefixes and suffixes.

Use new words in conversations: If you learn new words without using them, you will likely forget them in no time. However, when chatting with people or writing an email, sprinkle some of these new words into your writing. Gradually, they will become more ingrained in your memory and help you to build an impressive vocabulary list.

Learn a new word daily: This may seem daunting. However, it is a great learning tip. Make sure that a day does not go by without learning a new word. If you stick to this religiously, you will end up learning over 300 words in a year. Do this for five years, and your vocabulary list will have increased by around 1,000 words. That will have a significant impact on your reading and comprehension ability.

If you desire to improve your vocabulary by learning a word a day, you have several resources at your disposal. Some of these are A Word A Day, Wordnik, Merriam-Webster, WordReference.com, Vocabulary.com, the *New York Times*, Dictionary.com and Oxford.com. Most of these resources have Word of the Day features that teach you a word each day for as long as you have the app on your mobile device or follow these resources online. You can take advantage of these resources to keep learning and improving your vocabulary.

How to Make Inferences from Reading Material

Inference refers to the process of drawing conclusions from material based on your experience and previous knowledge of the subject matter. When you take a comprehension test, chances are that you will come across inference questions. Note that not all questions will require you to make inferences. To know whether it is necessary to infer, look for questions with words such as *imply, suggest* and *infer*. Also consider vocabulary, descriptions, supporting details and dialogue.

Next, put the identified details together to gain a better understanding of the material. Your inference must be supported by ideas or evidence explained in the passage. Otherwise, you may arrive at the wrong conclusion.

Practice regularly. You cannot just wake up and develop this skill. You can develop your ability to make logical inferences from texts by devoting hours of your time to practicing it regularly. Your hours of determination and dedication will pay off over time as you improve your ability to read between the lines and draw logical conclusions.

Craft, Structure and Language Skills

Your ability to explore the structure of a text will be tested in this section of the reading examination. The test is designed to determine whether you can establish a connection between the different parts of a text and determine its meaning. The organization of a reading text is also important.

Some questions require you to understand the literal meanings of words. This is one of the reasons why a dictionary and a thesaurus should be your friends. If you really do not know the exact meaning of a particular word, the context may provide some clues that will help you out. By *context*, we mean the surrounding words, examples and illustrations.

There are five types of context clues:

1. **Restatement/Synonym Clues:** These clues provide the synonym of a word in the same sentence. Consider the following example:

- *The principal was cantankerous, and very difficult to deal with.*
  The meaning of the word *cantankerous* has been provided by the succeeding words.

2. **Definition/Explanation Clues:** As the name implies, this type of clue provides a further explanation about a specific word that enables you to

understand the unfamiliar word. Such explanations are usually provided immediately after the word in question.
Consider the following example:

- *The little girl is ambidextrous—she can use both hands effortlessly.*
Even if you haven't heard the word *ambidextrous* before or do not know its meaning, the explanation gives you a clue into what the word means.

3. **Inference/General Clues:** If you are struggling with understanding a phrase or a word, look for clues before, after or within the sentence in which the unfamiliar phrase or word appears. You may even find the clue in the succeeding paragraph if you look carefully.
4. **Punctuation:** Punctuation marks provide clues into the meaning of a word or a phrase. For instance, if you are familiar with quotation marks, you will understand the meaning of a quoted word in a sentence because the meaning implied by the quotation may differ from its dictionary meaning.
Consider the following example:

- *Connor is a 'machine.'*
Connor is probably a human, so how can he also be a machine? The quotation marks tell you it's an idiomatic expression—probably referring to something like Connor's work ethic or maybe his sports abilities.
Dashes, apostrophes, parentheses and brackets are also used to explain the meaning of words. In this example, "The little girl is ambidextrous—she can use both hands effortlessly," the dash introduces the explanation of the word *ambidextrous*.

5. **Contrast/Antonym Clues:** An author may explain the meaning of a difficult word by providing its opposite. For instance, consider the following example:

- *Although the billionaire lives affluently now, he came from a poor background.*
Even if you do not understand the meaning of *affluently*, you probably understand what *poor* means. The contrast drawn between the billionaire's life then and now gives you a hint into the meaning of *affluently*.

Aside from helping you understand the meanings of difficult words, context can also help you identify the specific meaning of a polysemous word—a word that has multiple meanings.

An example is "He touched the pupil." In this example, it is difficult to pinpoint the meaning of *pupil*. The question is whether the man touched an eye or a student. The context will furnish you with information that will clear up that ambiguity.

For instance, *pupil* has different meanings in these sentences: "The pupil was late for the test" and "He touched the pupil of his eye." Thanks to the context, the different meanings stand out.

Bank, *get* and *man* are some examples of polysemy. So, before you jump to conclusions about the meaning of a seemingly familiar word, consider the context first.

Textual Organization

Sometimes, you may have to analyze a text's structure by focusing on how some parts of the text are related to other parts. While trying to understand a text's organization, the following questions will be helpful.

- How did the author build the argument? Ask this after identifying the text's main ideas.
- Which of the ideas did the author put first, and why?
- How did the author connect the first idea with other important points in the material?
- What about the main points? Do they follow a logical timeline or sequence?
- How is the material divided into sections?
- Did the author use compare and contrast to explain the similarities and differences between things, events or characters in the material?

If you can answer these questions satisfactorily, you will understand the author's organizational technique. That is another window into the material's overall message.

For a comprehensive analysis of the material, you may take a look into the writing tone by asking some relevant questions, such as:

- What tone did the author use?
- Did he use clear language?
- Does the author's use of words reveal if he has particular biases?

Content analysis is also important. This analysis will help you determine the format the author used to convey his message to the readers. This may include visual aids and other tools that may make it easier for the author to communicate with the audience.

For comprehensive content analysis, the following questions will be of help:

- Who is the author's target audience?
- What is the author's motive for writing the material?
- How did the author support the argument?
- What is the material's context?

As you find answers to each of these questions, the content will become clearer and easier to understand.

Integration of Knowledge and Ideas

Argument Analysis

Argument analysis involves breaking an author's argument down and analyzing it critically with a view to understanding the main idea better. The following tips will help you analyze an argument critically.

- Read the argument carefully and ensure that you understand it well. Does the argument have conclusions, claims and underlying assumptions? Identify these if they exist.
- What evidence is provided in the argument? What assumptions are made? What are the author's conclusions? These questions will give you an insight into the argument and improve your understanding.
- How does the author make logical connections in the argument? For a clue, look for words like *evidently*, *however*, *in conclusion*, *therefore*, *thus* and *hence*.
- After understanding the argument and identifying its major elements, think of the counterexamples and alternative explanations you can come up with. Is there additional evidence that may lend support to the argument or weaken it?
- And finally, after analyzing the argument, determine what changes can be made to the argument to increase its soundness.

The Effect of Evidence on Argument

An argument is considered a failure if the evidence is not strong enough to support it. So, how do you determine whether a piece of evidence is good or bad?

The most important factor to consider when analyzing a piece of evidence is its accuracy or truthfulness. How true is the evidence? Is it reliable? If the piece of evidence lacks these qualities, its ability to support the argument is flawed.

Three important factors must be considered before the accuracy or truthfulness of an argument can be determined:

Sufficiency: Ask yourself whether the evidence is sufficient to convince you of its accuracy. Individual judgment comes into play when determining whether evidence is sufficient. However, your knowledge about the topic and your ability to make logical inferences and assumptions will go a long way in helping you determine whether the available evidence is sufficient or not.

Relevance: Relevance is another factor that is crucial to an accurate assessment of the available evidence. A piece of evidence is considered relevant if you can establish a definite relationship between the evidence and the claim. This shows that a relationship must exist, although it is not mandatory for the relationship to be well defined or direct. However, the clearer and more direct the relationship, the better. If a piece of evidence is absolutely accurate but has zero relationship with the claim, the evidence is worthless.

Representation: You should also ask yourself if the evidence is representative or not. A piece of evidence is said to be representative if it does justice to the material's portrayal without distorting the point under discussion or supporting a section of the material. This is the most difficult and most important factor you must consider when doing this analysis.

For instance, if in an attempt to prove that school drop-outs are successful, an author cites Mark Zuckerberg and Bill Gates as examples, the author hasn't done justice to that argument. Zuckerberg and Gates are a fraction of school drop-outs, and a higher percentage of such individuals struggle to pay their bills. Thus, while the examples are accurate, they distort the point under discussion because they do not represent the financial status of an average drop-out.

Chapter Two: Mathematics

Numbers and Quantity

Whole numbers are countable numbers, such as 1, 2, 3, 4 and so on. Numbers such as 123, 6,790 and 10,235 are examples of whole numbers. Note that these are positive numbers. Negative numbers are not whole numbers.

Some other classes of numbers are discussed below.

Integers

Integers include both positive and negative numbers, but they don't include fractions. Zero is also an integer.

Decimals

Decimal numbers are numbers with a whole part and a fractional part. Some examples of decimals are 23.45, 0.89 and 56.78. The numbers before the decimal point are the whole number, while the numbers after the decimal numbers are the fractional parts.

Just as you can perform mathematical operations on integers, you can do the same on decimal numbers. This section covers all the operations you can perform on decimals, starting with addition.

Fractions

A fraction is a non-whole number with a numerator and a denominator. In the expression 2/4, 3 is the numerator while 4 is the denominator.

Types of Fractions

There are three types of fractions: proper, improper and mixed.

In **proper fractions**, the numerator is smaller than the denominator. Some examples of proper fractions are 2/3, 7/9 and 11/15.

In **improper fractions**, the numerator is bigger than the numerator. Examples of improper fractions are 4/3, 7/6 and 9/2.

Mixed fractions contain a whole part and a fraction. Examples of mixed fractions are 1 1/2 and 8 1/2. Improper fractions can be converted into mixed fractions.

Conversion of Improper Fraction to Mixed Fraction

When dealing with fractions, improper fractions are not acceptable as the final answer, unless indicated by the examiner. This may require you to convert the improper fraction to a mixed fraction. Here are some examples to explain the conversion:

Example 1

Convert 7/5 to an improper fraction.

Solution:

Step 1: How many times can 5 divide 7?

Step 2: Find the remainder.

Step 3: Write the number of division times as the whole number and the remainder as the numerator. The denominator remains unchanged.

In 7/5, 5 can divide 7 only once. The remainder is 2. Following the rule, the whole number is 1; the numerator is 2 and the denominator is 5. Hence, 7/5 = 1 2/5.

Example 2

Convert 22/7 into a mixed fraction.

Solution:

Step 1: How many times can 7 divide 22?

Step 2: Find the remainder.

Step 3: Write the number of division times as the whole number and the remainder as the numerator. The denominator remains unchanged.

How many times can 7 divide 22? 7 can divide 22 three times. The remainder is 1. Thus, the whole number is 3; the numerator is 3 and the denominator is 7. Hence 22/7 = 3 1/7.

It is noteworthy that every mathematical operation that can be performed on integers can also be performed on fractions. We will consider some of these operations below, starting with the addition of fractions.

Addition of Fractions

To add two or more fractions, you must find a common multiple of both denominators. For instance, if the denominators of two fractions are 4 and 5, you must find a number that can be divided by both 4 and 5. For smaller numbers, you may decide to multiply the denominators to arrive at their common multiple. For 4 and 5, 20 is a common multiple if you multiply the two denominators.

However, sometimes there may be a common multiple of the denominators that is smaller than the multiple of both numbers. For instance, if the denominators are 3 and 6, you will get 18 as the common multiple if you multiply the two numbers. However, since 6 is a multiple of 3, you will do fine with 6 as the common multiple. Thus, before you multiply the two numbers when finding a common multiple, try to find a smaller number that will make your work a lot easier.

Example 1

Find the sum of 2/3 and 4/5.

Solution:

Step 1: Find a common multiple of the denominators.

For 3 and 5, the smallest common multiple is 15.

Step 2: Proceed with the addition.

2/3 + 4/5 = [(5 * 2) + (3 * 4)]/15 = (10 + 12)/ 15 = 22/15. Note that this is an improper fraction and should be converted to proper fractions.

Hence, 22/15 = 1 7/15.

However, how did we arrive at the answer?

For the first section of the equation, 2/3, how many times can 3 divide 15? The answer is 5. Then, multiply the numerator, 2, by 5. That gives 5 * 2, or 10.

For the second section, 4/5, how many times can 5 divide 15? The answer is 3. Multiply the numerator, 4, by 3. That gives 3 * 4, or 12.

You can now add both sections together to get the numerator while the denominator is 15, their common multiple.

Example 2

Find the sum of 3/7 and 1/3.

Solution:

Step 1: Identify the common multiple of 7 and 3.

The simplest multiple of both numbers is 21.

Step 2: Proceed with the addition.

3/7 + 1/3 = [(3 * 3) + (7 * 1)]/21 = (9 + 8)/21.

(9 +8)/21 = 17/21.

See if you can simplify the answer further. Since both 17 and 21 do not have common factors, they are indivisible. Therefore, 3/7 + 1/3 = 17/21.

Subtraction of Fractions

Now let's consider how fractions can be subtracted from each other.

Example 1

Subtract 1/2 from 4/5.

Solution:

Step 1: Rearrange the numbers and subtract the smaller number from the bigger number.

Step 2: Find the common multiple of 2 and 5.

Step 3: Proceed with the subtraction.

Thus, 4/5 – 1/2 = [(2 * 4) – (5 * 1)]/10 = (8 – 5)/10.

(8 – 5)/10 = 3/10

Example 2

Subtract 4/5 from 9/10.

Solution:

Step 1: Rearrange the numbers and subtract the smaller number from the bigger number.

Step 2: Find the common multiple of 5 and 10.

Step 3: Proceed with the subtraction.

Thus, 9/10 – 4/5 = [(1 * 9) – (2 * 4)]/10 = (9 – 8)/10.

(9 – 8)/10 = 1/10

Subtraction of fractions can be difficult. This is because it may be challenging to know which of the two fractions is bigger and which is smaller. Without this knowledge, you will either be unable to perform the subtraction operation or might arrive at the wrong answer.

To overcome this problem, convert both numbers to decimals. The bigger decimal value is the bigger fraction.

Division of Fractions

You can divide fractions with a whole number or a fraction. To divide a fraction with any given number, multiply the fraction by the inverse of the divisor. Then simplify the expression after the multiplication if necessary.

Example 1

Divide 3/4 by 4.

Solution:

Step 1: Find the inverse of the divisor. In this question, the inverse of 4 is 1/4.

Step 2: Multiply the number by the inverse.

Thus, 3/4 divided by 4 = 3/4 * 1/4.3/4 *1/4 = 3/16.

Example 2

Divide 2/7 by 1/3.

Solution:

Step 1: Find the inverse of the divisor. In this question, the inverse of 4 is 1/4.

Step 2: Multiply the number by the inverse.

In the given expression, the inverse of 1/3 is 3/1, or 3. Thus, to divide 2/7 by 1/3, multiply 2/7 by 3/1.

2/7 divided by 1/3 = 2/7 * 3/1 = 6/7.

Multiplication of Fractions

Multiplication of fractions is a straightforward process. You simply multiply the fraction by the multiplier, either a whole number or a fraction.

Example 1

Multiply 2/5 by 2.

Solution:

Step 1: Multiply the fraction directly by the multiplier.

2/5 multiplied by 2 = 2/5 * 2/1.

2/5 * 2/1 = 4/5.

Example 2

Multiply 3/4 by 1/2.

Solution: 3/4 multiplied by 1/2 =3/4 * 1/23/4 *1/2 = 3/8

Be careful when dividing and multiplying fractions because both involve multiplying the given fraction by the divisor or multiplier. However, while you multiply the number by the inverse of the divisor, you multiply the fraction directly by the multiplier, not its inverse.

Fraction-to-Decimal Conversion

To convert a fraction to a decimal, divide the numerator by the denominator until you are through with the division.

Example 1

Convert 3/4 to a decimal.

Solution:

How many times can 4 divide 3? It cannot. That's 0. You then add 0 to 3 to become 30.

How many times can 4 divide 30? The answer is 7. 4 * 7 = 28. So, 30 – 28 = 2. The remainder is 2. We then add 0 to the 2 to become 20.

How many times can 4 divide 20? The answer is 5, without a remainder. Then take 7 and 5 and put them together, then shift the decimal place to the left twice, so 75.0 → 0.75.

3/4 = 0.75.

Example 2

Convert 2/3 to a decimal.

Solution:

How many times can 3 go into 2? 0 times. Then, add 0 to the 2 to become 20. How many times can 3 divide 20? The answer is 6. 6 * 3 = 18. 20 – 18 = 2. You add 0 to the number to become 20 and repeat the process.

Note that this division will go to infinity. Stop the division when you are satisfied with the result.

Hence, 2/3 = 0.66666666, or 0.67 to two decimal places. We will discuss the rounding off of numbers later in the book.

Ratios and Proportions

Ratios deal with the comparison of two numbers or quantities. They are used to define how many times a specific number is contained in another given number. The ratio of two numbers, a and b, can be written as a:b or a/b.

Some of the operations that can be performed on ratios include scaling, equaling, reduction and word problems.

Scaling a Ratio

Scaling a ratio is a mathematical operation that involves multiplying the ratio values by a specific number known as the scaling value. The scaling value is determined by the question.

Example 1

If a fashion designer needs 3 yards to sew cloth for a young man, how many yards does she need to sew the same style for 4 young men?

Solution:

For 1 man, the ratio of the yard to people is 1:3.

For 4 young men, multiply the value by 4.

= (1:3) * 4 = 4:12

The tailor needs 12 yards of cloth to sew the same style for 4 young men.

Example 2

If there are 15 boys and 10 girls in a class, how many girls and boys are in 4 classes?

Solution:

Boys : girls for 1 class = 15:10

For 4 classes, multiply the ratio by 4.

4 classes = (15:10) * 4

4 classes = 60:40.

Hence, there are 60 boys and 40 girls divided among 4 classes.

Equal Ratios

Ratios are said to be equal if they have the same value. Such ratios are otherwise known as equivalent ratios. To test if two ratios are equal or equivalent, multiply or divide them by the same value.

Example 1

Find the equivalent ratio of 2/3.

Solution:

To find the equivalent ratio, multiply it by any number. Let's pick 4.

Thus, (2/3) * 4 = 8/12.

Example 2

The ratio of goats to sheep in a garden is 4/7. Find the equivalent ratio.

Solution:

Multiply the ratio by any number of your choice. Let's say 3.

(4/7) * 3 = 12/21.

Hint: When you are asked to test the equality of two ratios, convert them to decimals. If their decimal values are the same, they are equal ratios.

Ratio Reduction

Ratio reduction requires you to reduce a ratio to the lowest form. This is possible if the components of the ratio have a common factor.

Example 1

Reduce 12/15 to the lowest form.

Solution:

The given ratio: 12/15

Divide the ratio by its common factor. In this case, 12 and 15 are multiples of 3. Thus, divide through by 3.

Hence, 12/15 = 4/5 if you divide the ratio by the common factor.

Example 2

Simplify 36:42.

Solution:

The principle is the same: find a common divisor for the ratio. As you can see, both figures are multiples of 6. Hence, divide through by 6.

36/6:42/6 = 6:7.

Word Problems Involving Ratios

Sometimes, problems involving ratios are not expressed in algebra but in words. If you can break the words down, you can easily solve the ratio problems, as shown in these examples.

Example 1

If a man spends $50 out of his $150 income on food and gas, what ratio of his income does he spend on gas and food?

Solution:

Total income: $150

Expenses on food and gas: $50

Ratio of income to expenses is $150:$50. Divide through by $50.

$150:$50 = $150/$50: $50/$50 = 3:1

Therefore, the ratio of the man's income to his expenses is 3:1.

Example 2

While driving, Jane realized she has just completed 20 miles of her 100-mile journey. What fraction of her journey does she still have to complete?

Solution:

Total distance: 100 miles

Distance covered: 20 miles

Distance left = total distance – distance covered = 100 miles – 20 miles = 80 miles

Fraction of distance to be covered = total distance:distance left

= 100 miles:80 miles. Divide through by 20 miles.

100 miles/20 miles: 80 miles/20 miles = 5:4. Thus, Jane is yet to cover 4/5 of her journey.

Proportion involves the comparison of two values to establish if they are equal in value or not. To determine the proportionality of two values, cross-multiply them. If one side of the equation equals the other side of the equation, the two values are equal.

Example 1

Determine the proportionality of 4/5 and 10/12.

Solution:

Step 1: Rewrite the equation.

4:5 = 10:12

Step 2: Cross-multiply the values.

4 * 12 = 48

5 * 10 = 50

Since 48 is not equal to 50, the values 4/5 and 10/12 are not proportional.

Note: When you are multiplying two ratios to determine their proportionality, multiply the middle, or mean, terms together and the outer, or extremes, together.

Thus, to determine if a:b = c:d, multiply b by c and a by d. Determine if ad = bc.

Example 2

Find the value of y 3/4 proportional to y/20.

Solution:

Rewrite the ratios.

3:4= y:20

Cross-multiply the ratios.

3 * 20 = 4 * y

60 = 4y

Since the ratios are proportional, 4y = 60

To find the value of y, divide both sides of the equation by 4.

(4y)/4 = 60/y

x = 15

Hence, for the ratio 3/4 and y/20 to be proportional, y = 15.

Percentages

Sometimes, numbers are expressed in percentages. When they are, they are expressed in relation to 100. When you see expressions like 30%, 70% and so on, they simply mean 30 out of 100 and 70 out of 100, respectively.

Some examples will clarify this.

Example 1

In a bus of 50 passengers, 20 are female while the rest are male. Express the male passengers as a percentage of the total passengers.

Solution:

Number of passengers on the bus: 50

Number of female passengers: 20

Number of male passengers: x

Step 1: First, calculate the number of male passengers in the vehicle.

Number of male passengers = total number of passengers – number of female passengers.

Number of male passengers = 50 passengers – 20 passengers = 30 passengers.

Step 2: Express the number of male passengers as a fraction of the total number of passengers and multiply it by 100.

= (30 passengers /50 passengers) * 100 = 0.6 * 100 = 60%.

Hence, male passengers make up 60% of the total number of passengers on the bus.

Example 2

Express 12/15 as a percentage.

Solution:

There are two ways to solve this problem. Method one involves multiplying the ratio by 100 and simplifying the result, while the second method involves converting the ratio to decimals and multiplying the result by 100.

Method 1

12/15 as a percentage = (12/15) * 100 = 1,200/15

1,200/15 = 80

Thus, 12/15 = 80%.

Method 2

12/15 as a percentage = (12/15) * 100 = 0.8 * 100

Thus, 0.8 * 100 = 80.

Therefore, 12/15 = 100%.

As you can see, irrespective of the method you use, you will always get the same answers if your calculations are right.

Conversion

Conversion is important for measurements, such as length, area and volume. It also involves the conversion of rates such as gallons per mile, miles per hour, cubic feet per minute and other relevant conversions.

Below are some conversion units you can use to convert one metric unit to another.

1 pound = 0.4536 kilograms

1 square meter = 10.76 square feet

1 meter = 100 centimeters

0.6214 mile = 1 kilometer

2.2046 pounds = 1 kilogram

1 mile = 1.609 kilometers

1 foot = 30.38 centimeters

Let's see some practical applications of these conversion units.

Example 1

A vehicle was weighed in kilograms. If it weighed 8,000 kilograms, what is the weight in pounds?

Solution:

Vehicle's weight = 1,800 kilograms

1 kilogram = 2.2046 pounds

Thus, 1,800 kilograms = 1,800 * 2.2046 pounds = 3,968.28 pounds.

Example 2

Convert 2,000 miles to kilometers.

Solution:

Distance = 2,000 miles

1 mile = 1.609 kilometers

Thus, 2,000 miles = 2,000 * 1.609 = 3,218 kilometers.

Example 3

During a competition, cyclists covered 10,000 kilometers. What is the distance the cyclists covered in miles?

Solution:

Distance covered = 10,000 kilometers

1.609 kilometers = 1 mile

To convert 10,000 kilometers to miles, divide it by 1.609.

10,000 kilometers to miles = (10,000/1.609) miles = 6,215 miles.

Rounding of Numbers

During calculations, rounding numbers may be necessary. How do you go about this?

Rounding Number to the Nearest 10

Rounding a number to the nearest 10 is one of the most common rounding operations. When performing this rounding operation, bear this simple general rule in mind:

If the number is between 0 and 4, it will be rounded down to zero. Numbers between 5 and 9 are rounded up to 10. The rule applies to every last digit in a number.

Example 1

Round 1,234 to the nearest 10.

Solution:

Step 1: Determine whether the last digit is between 1 and 4 or between 5 and 9.

Step 2: Round the last digit down to 0 if it's less than 5 and up to 10 if it's between 5 and 9.

In the given problem, the last digit is 4 and therefore will be rounded down to 0. Hence, 1,234 = 1,230 to the nearest 10.

Example 2

Round 456 to the nearest 10.

Solution:

Step 1: Determine whether the last digit is between 1 and 4 or between 5 and 9.

Step 2: Round the last digit down to 0 if it's less than 5 and up to 10 if it's between 5 and 9.

The last digit in 456 is 6 and should be rounded up to 10. Add the 10 to the remaining 450 to get 460.

Therefore, 456 to the nearest 10 is 460.

Rounding Numbers to the Nearest 100

Numbers between 1 and 49 are rounded down to 0, and numbers between 50 and 99 are rounded up to 100.

In bigger numbers, consider the last two digits of the number and apply the principle.

Example 1

Round 456 to nearest 100.

Solution:

Step 1: Check the last two digits.

Step 2: Round them down to 0 if they are below 50 and up to 100 if they are between 50 and 99.

In 456, the last two digits are 56. Round the number up to 100 and add it to the remaining 400.

400 + 100 = 500. Hence, 456 to the nearest 100 is 500.

Example 2

Round 5,627 to the nearest 100.

Step 1: Check the last two digits.

Step 2: Round them down to 0 if they are below 50 and up to 100 if they are between 50 and 99.

The given number is 5,627, and the last two digits are 27.

Since 27 is below 50, the number will be rounded down to 0 and added to the left, for 5,600.

Thus, 5,627 to the nearest 100 is 5,600.

Rounding Decimal Numbers

Rounding is not limited to whole numbers; decimal numbers can also be rounded. You can round to tenths, hundredths, thousandths and so on. Sometimes, you may have to round decimal numbers to a specific number of significant figures.

The general principle for decimal rounding stipulates that you must leave a single number after the decimal point if you are rounding to tenths, two digits if you are rounding to the hundredths and so on.

Then, you can round the remaining numbers as you deem fit according to the rules governing rounding of whole numbers, starting from the last digit to the right.

Example 1

Round 87.324 to the nearest tenth.

Solution:

Step 1: Start rounding from the last digit on the right and move to the left.

Step 2: Round numbers below 5 down and numbers between 5 and 9 up.

The last number is 4. It will be rounded down to 0. Same applies to the next number, 2.

Thus, 87.324 is 87.3 to the nearest tenth.

Example 2

Round 23.467 to two decimal places.

Solution:

This is similar to nearest hundredth.

Step 1: Ensure you keep to the two numbers-after-the-decimal-point rule.

Step 2: Check the last digit for rounding up or down.

In the given problem, 7 is the last digit and will be rounded up. Thus, 23.467 to two decimal places is 23.48.

Rounding Decimals to Significant Digits

Decimal numbers can also be rounded to a specific number of significant digits. However, the rule is simple: count the number of specified significant digits before you start rounding up or down.

Example 1

Round 23.456 to four significant digits.

Solution:

Step 1: Count four digits from the left.

Step 2: Start rounding from the last number and stop at the fifth number.

The first four digits in 23.456 are 23.45. Round the last digit, 6, up to 1 and add it to the fourth digit.

Thus, 23.456 is 23.46 to four significant digits.

Example 2

Round 0.045678 to two significant digits.

Solution:

As usual, you count two digits from the left before you start rounding. Note that the trailing zeros are insignificant and should be discarded when counting the real digits.

So, the first two digits are 45. Start rounding up from 8, the last digit.

Since 8 is more than 5, it is rounded up to 1. The 1 is added to the next digit to its left, 7. That becomes 8.

Round the 8 up to 1 and add it to the next digit to the left, 6, to become 7. 7 is a bigger number than 5 and should be rounded up to 1 and added to the next digit. When you round the 7 up, add it to 5 to give you 6.

Therefore, 0.045678 = 0.046 to two significant figures.

Algebra

Rather than regular expressions, algebra uses symbols to represent values. The relationship between two variables is usually shown by algebraic equations. Some examples of algebraic expressions are 5ab + 3bc, 10xy and ab + c.

Some common terms in algebra are *coefficients, like terms* and *unlike terms*. Coefficients are numbers that prefix algebraic expressions. For instance, in the expression 4ab + 5ac, 4 and 5 are the coefficients of ab and ac, respectively.

Like terms are algebraic expressions with the same variables, while unlike terms are expressions whose variables are different. While ab + 3ab are like terms, 3ab + 4xy are unlike. This is because while ab is the variable in the former, the variable in the latter is xy. Thus, these variables are dissimilar, constituting unlike terms.

Algebraic expressions create room for mathematical operations that are performed on whole numbers. Let's consider the major operations, such as subtraction, addition, division and multiplication.

Addition in Algebra

When adding two algebraic expressions, you cannot add two expressions with different variables.

Example 1

Find the sum of 2ab + 4xy + xy + 8ab.

Solution:

From the equation, you can identify two like terms with two variables, ab and xy.

Step 1: Rearrange the question.

2ab + 4xy + xy + 8ab = 2ab + 8ab + 4xy + xy

Step 2: Add the like terms.

2ab + 8ab + 4xy + xy = 10ab + 5xy

Thus, the sum of 2ab + 8ab + 4xy + xy = 10ab + 5xy.

Example 2

Add 5bc + 8 cd + 3ay +3bc + 2ay + 2xy.

Solution:

From the equation, you can identify some like terms and unlike terms.

Step 1: Rearrange the question.

5bc + 8 cd + 3ay +3bc + 2ay + 2xy = 5bc + 3bc + 8cd + 3ay + 2ay + 2xy

Step 2: Add the like terms.

5bc + 3bc + 8cd + 3ay + 2ay + 2xy = 8bc + 8cd + 5ay + 2xy

Therefore, 5bc + 8 cd + 3ay +3bc + 2ay + 2xy = 8bc + 8cd + 5ay + 2xy.

Subtraction of Algebraic Expressions

There is no difference between a regular subtraction operation in whole numbers and algebra. You need to pay attention to like and unlike terms and rearrange the given problem to reflect these terms before proceeding with the subtraction.

Example 1

Simplify the expression 8ab + 3bc + 10xy – 2ab – 4xy.

Solution:

Step 1: Identify the like and unlike terms and rearrange the question accordingly.

8ab + 3bc + 10xy – 2ab – 4xy = 8ab – 2ab + 3bc + 10xy – 4xy

Step 2: Proceed with the subtraction.

8ab – 2ab + 3bc + 10xy – 4xy = 6ab + 3bc + 6xy

Therefore, 8ab + 3bc + 10xy – 2ab -4xy = 6ab + 3bc + 6xy.

Example 2

Subtract 2bc + 5xy from 10bc + 7xy.

Solution:

Step 1: Rearrange the question.

= (10bc + 7xy) – (2bc + 5xy)

Step 2: Open the parentheses.

(10bc + 7xy) – (2bc + 5xy) = 10bc + 7xy – 2bc – 5xy

Step 3: Rearrange the expression.

10bc + 7xy – 2bc – 5xy = 10bc – 2bc + 7xy – 5xy

10bc – 2bc + 7xy – x5y = 8bc + 2xy

Therefore, (10bc + 7xy) – (2bc + 5xy) = 8bc + 2xy.

Note that the numbers in the second parentheses are all affected by the negative sign when opening the parentheses. Thus, you must pay attention when opening a parenthesis to ensure that the numbers have the right positive or negative sign before you proceed with your operation.

Division in Algebra

Division in algebra can be tricky. The examples below show how to divide algebraic expressions.

Example 1

Divide 20xy by 5xy.

Solution:

Step 1: Rearrange the equation.

20xy divided by 5xy = 20xy/5xy

Step 2: Simplify the expression.

Note that 20 is a multiply of 5 and thus can be divided by 5. More so, both the numerator and the denominator contain xy. So these variables will cancel each other out.

Thus, 20xy/5xy = 4.

Example 2

Divide 12cd by 4d.

Solution:

Step 1: Rearrange the equation.

12cd divided by 4d = 12cd/4d

Step 2: Simplify the expression.

Note that 12 is a multiple of 4 and can be divided by 4. Also, while the numerator contains cd, the denominator contains d. The d in the denominator will cancel out the d in the numerator.

Hence, 12cd/4d = 3c.

Multiplication in Algebra

You can multiply an algebraic equation by another one to get a third algebraic expression.

Example 1

Multiply (a + 2) by (a + 3).

Solution:

Step 1: Open the first parentheses and use its contents to multiply the second parentheses.

(a + 2) * (a + 3) = a (a + 3) + 2 (a + 3).

= a (a + 3) + 2 (a + 3) = (a^2 + 3a) + (2a + 6)

Step 2: Open the two parentheses.

(a^2 + 3a) + (2a + 6) = a^2 + 3a + 2a + 6

Step 3: Simplify the expression.

a^2 + 3a + 2a + 6 = a^2 + 5a + 6

Example 2

Multiply (a – 4) by (a + 3).

Solution:

Step 1: Open the first parentheses and use its contents to multiply the second parentheses.

Hence, $(a - 4) * (a + 3) = a (a + 3) - 4(a + 3)$.

$= a (a + 3) - 4 (a + 3) = (a^2 + 3a) - (-a - 12)$

Step 2: Open the two parentheses.

$(a^2 + 3a) - (4a - 12) = a^2 + 3a - 4a - 12$

Step 3: Simplify the expression.

$a^2 + 3a - 4a - 12 = a^2 - a - 12$

Geometric Shapes

Geometric shapes are divided into two-dimensional shapes and three-dimensional shapes.

Two-Dimensional Shapes

Two-dimensional shapes have two measurable dimensions, namely the length and the width.

Some examples of two-dimensional shapes are circles, squares, quadrilaterals, triangles, rectangles and pentagons.

Three-Dimensional Shapes

Three-dimensional shapes have measurable width, length and depth or height. Some examples are spheres, cuboids, pyramids, cubes, cones and cylinders.

Properties of Geometric Shapes

Geometric shapes have distinct properties that distinguish one shape from another. Some geometric shapes and their features are listed below.

Square

A square is a geometrical shape with four right angles, four equal sides and four lines of symmetry. Squares are members of the rectangle and rhombus families. They are also considered parallelograms.

Trapezoid

A trapezoid is a quadrilateral formed when the top of a triangle is removed. While most quadrilaterals have parallel sides, one pair of a trapezoid's sides are parallel, while the other pair are not parallel. The base of the trapezoid is the parallel side.

Rectangle

A rectangle has four right angles, four sides and two lines of symmetry. It is a parallelogram. Two opposite sides of a rectangle are equal in length.

Rhombus

The opposite sides of a rhombus are parallel, while all four sides are equal in size. Rhombuses have two lines of symmetry, which can be four lines if the rhombus is a square. Rhombuses are also parallelograms.

Polygons

Polygons are named by their number of sides. Three-sided polygons are known as triangles, while four-sided polygons are referred to as quadrilaterals. Some examples of quadrilaterals are squares, rectangles, parallelograms, rhombuses, kites and trapezoids. Pentagons and hexagons are five-sided and six-sided polygons, respectively. A heptagon has seven sides; an octagon has eight sides; a nonagon has nine sides and a decagon has 10 sides.

Triangle

There are different types of triangles. These include scalene triangles, obtuse triangles, equilateral triangles, isosceles right-angle triangles and acute triangles.

Isosceles triangles are triangles with two equal sides and angles. A line of symmetry is a common feature of this type of triangle, while scalene triangles are triangles without equal lengths or angles.

Obtuse triangles have one of their angles greater than 90 degrees; the other two angles are acute, or less than 90 degrees. In acute angles, all the angles are less than 90 degrees.

In right triangles, one angle is a right angle, or 90 degrees. Note that the sum of the angles of a triangle is 180 degrees, or two right angles.

The Pythagorean Theorem

The Pythagorean Theorem explains the relationship between the three sides of a right-angle triangle. The theorem states that the square of the hypotenuse side of a right-angle triangle is equal to the sum of the squares of the other sides of the triangle.

The two other sides of the triangle are known as the base and the perpendicular. The longest side of a right-angle triangle is the hypotenuse. It is opposite to the triangle's 90-degree side.

In a right-angle triangle with base a, perpendicular b and hypotenuse c, the Pythagorean Theorem states that $c^2 = a^2 + b^2$. Thus, $c = \sqrt{a^2 + b^2}$.

Example 1

Find the size of the hypotenuse of a right-angle triangle with a 3 cm base and a 4 cm perpendicular.

Solution:

Base of triangle, a = 3 cm

Perpendicular of triangle, b = 4 cm

Hypotenuse $c = \sqrt{a^2 + b^2}$

$C = \sqrt{3^2 + 4^2} = \sqrt{9 + 16}$

$\sqrt{9 + 16} = \sqrt{25} = 5$

Thus, the hypotenuse side of the triangle is 5 cm.

Example 2

Calculate the base of a right-angle triangle if the hypotenuse is 10 cm and the perpendicular is 6 cm.

Solution:

Base of the triangle = x

Perpendicular side of the triangle = 6 cm

Hypotenuse of the triangle = 10 cm

$h = \sqrt{b^2 + p^2}$. Thus, $10\text{cm} = \sqrt{x^2 + 6^2}$.

Square both sides.

$10^2 = (\sqrt{x^2 + 6^2})^2$

Thus, $100 = x^2 + 36$.

Organize the like terms.

$100 - 36 = x^2$ or $x^2 = 100 - 36$

$x^2 = 64$

Find the square root of both sides.

$\sqrt{x^2} = \sqrt{64}$

$x = 8$

Thus, the base of the triangle is 8 cm.

Example 3

Find the size of the perpendicular side of a right-angle triangle of hypotenuse with 8 cm and 5 cm bases, respectively.

Solution:

Hypotenuse a = 8 cm

Perpendicular b = x

Base c = 5 cm.

$a = \sqrt{c^2 + b^2}$

$8 = \sqrt{5^2 + b^2}$

$8 = \sqrt{25 + b^2}$

Square both sides.

$82 = (\sqrt{25 + b^2})^2$

$64 = 25 + b2$

Organize the like terms.

$b^2 = 64 - 25$

$b^2 = 39$

Find the square root of both sides.

$\sqrt{b^2} = \sqrt{39}$

$b = 6.25$

Hence, the perpendicular side of the triangle is 6.25 cm.

Pythagorean Triples

A Pythagorean triple is a type of right-angle triangle with all positive sides, such that the sides obey the general formula $c^2 = a^2 + b^2$.

In the three examples above, the first two examples form Pythagorean triples because all the sides are positive integers. The last example is not a Pythagorean triple because one of the sides is a decimal number. For a set of Pythagorean triples, all the sides must be whole numbers.

Some examples of Pythagorean triples are:

3, 4, 5

5, 12, 13

6, 8, 10

8, 15, 17.

Calculations Involving Geometric Shapes

Several calculations can be performed on geometric shapes. We will find the area, perimeter, circumference and volume of some of these shapes.

Area and Perimeter of a Square

The perimeter and area of a square are given by 4l and l^2, respectively, where l represents the length of each side of the square.

Example 1

Calculate the perimeter of a square with 5 cm sides.

Solution:

As previously mentioned, a square is a shape with all sides equal. Hence, both the width and the length of the square are 5 cm each.

The perimeter of a square, where the side is denoted by "a," can be calculated by multiplying a by 4, i.e., P= 4a.

Thus, the perimeter of the square of sides 5 cm = 4 * 5 cm = 20 cm.

Example 2

If a square has 10 cm sides, what is its perimeter?

Solution:

Side of the square, a = 10 cm

Perimeter of the square = 4a = 4 * 10 cm = 40 cm

Example 3

If the perimeter of a square is 50 cm, what is its length?

Solution:

Perimeter of the square, 4l = 50 cm

To find the side of the square, divide through by 4.

4l/4 = 50 cm/4

L = 12.5 cm

Thus, each side of the square is 12.5 cm in length.

Example 4

Calculate the area of a square with 8 cm sides.

Solution:

For a square of side l, the area of the square is given by $A = l^2$.

Thus, area of the square of sides 8 cm = $(8\text{ cm})^2 = 64\text{ cm}^2$.

Example 5

If the area of a square is 100 cm^2, how long is each side of the square?

Solution:

Area of a square of length l = l^2

Area of the square = 100 cm^2

$l^2 = 100\text{ cm}^2$

Find the square root of both sides.

$\sqrt{l^2} = \sqrt{100\text{ cm}^2}$

l = 10 cm

Therefore, each side of the square is 10 cm long.

Perimeter of a Triangle

The perimeter of a triangle can be calculated with the formula p = a + b + c, where a, b, and c are the three sides of the triangle.

Example 1

Calculate the perimeter of a triangle with sides that are 4, 7 and 8 centimeters.

Solution:

Perimeter of a triangle = a + b + c, where a, b, and c are 4 cm, 7 cm and 8 cm, respectively.

Therefore, P = 4 cm + 7 cm + 8 cm = 19 cm.

Example 2

If the perimeter of an isosceles triangle is 24 cm, what is the length of the triangle?

Solution:

Although this question seems tricky, it is actually straightforward if you understand the basic principle.

Note that the question is about an isosceles triangle. Thus, all sides are equal.

So, let's represent each side with x. All three sides are x + x + x, or 3x.

Perimeter of the triangle = 24 cm

Therefore, 24 cm = 3x.

Divide through by 3.

24 cm/3 = 3x/3

8 cm = x

Therefore, each side of the isosceles triangle is 8 cm long.

Area of a Triangle

The formula for calculating the area of a triangle is Area = 1/2 * b * h, where b and h are the width of the triangle and its height, respectively.

Example 1

Calculate the area of a triangle 10 cm high and 8 cm wide.

Solution:

Height of the triangle, h = 10 cm

Width of the triangle, b = 8 cm

Area = 1/2 * b * h = 1/2 * 8 cm * 10 cm

Area = 1/2 * 80 cm = 40 cm^2.

Example 2

A triangle is 20 cm from one side to the other and is 15 cm from the base to the top. Calculate its area.

Solution:

Width of the triangle, b = 20 cm

Height of the triangle, h = 15 cm

Area of the triangle = 1/2 * b * h

Area of the triangle = 1/2 * 20 cm * 15 cm

Area of the triangle = 1/2 * 300 cm^2 = 150 cm^2

Example 3

If the area of a triangle is 200 cm^2, what is its height if its base is 10 cm?

Solution:

Area of a triangle = 1/2 * b * h, where b and h are the base and height of the triangle, respectively.

200 cm^2 = 1/2 * b * h

200 cm^2 = 1/2 * 10 * h

200 cm^2 = 5h

Divide through by 5.

200 cm^2/5 = 5h/5

40 cm = h

Thus, the triangle is 40 cm tall.

Perimeter of a Parallelogram

To calculate the perimeter of a parallelogram, use the formula P = 2 (sum of the adjacent sides).

Example 1

Calculate the perimeter of a parallelogram of adjacent sides that are 10 cm and 15 cm long, respectively.

Solution:

Sum of the adjacent sides = 10 cm + 15 cm = 25 cm

Perimeter = 2 (sum of adjacent sides)

Perimeter = 2 (25 cm) = 50 cm

Example 2

What is the sum of the adjacent sides of a parallelogram if the perimeter of the triangle is 72 cm?

Solution:

Perimeter of a parallelogram = 2 * sum of adjacent sides

72 cm = 2 (sum of adjacent sides)

Divide through by 2.

72 cm/2 = 2(sum of adjacent sides)

36 cm = sum of adjacent sides.

Area of a Parallelogram

You can find the area of a parallelogram with the formula A = base * height.

Example 1

Find the area of a parallelogram with a 12 cm base and a 15 cm height.

Solution:

Base of parallelogram = 12 cm

Height of parallelogram = 15 cm

Area of parallelogram = base * height

Area of parallelogram = 12 cm * 15 cm = 180 cm^2.

Example 2

Find the height of a parallelogram with a 200 cm^2 area if the base of the parallelogram is 10 cm.

Solution:

Base of the parallelogram = 10 cm

Height of the parallelogram = x

Area of the parallelogram = 200 cm^2

Area of parallelogram = 10 cm * x

200 cm^2 = 10cm * x

Divide through by 10 cm.

200 cm^2/10cm = 10x cm/10 cm

20 cm = x

Therefore, the parallelogram is 20 cm tall.

Area of a Circle

The area of a circle of radius r can be calculated by the formula $A = \pi r^2$. For a circle of diameter d, the radius is r = d/2. π = 22/7, or 3.142.

Example 1

Calculate the area of a circle of radius 7 cm, given that π = 22/7.

Solution:

Area of circle = πr^2

Area of the circle = (22/7) * 7 cm * 7 cm

Area of the circle = 22 * 7 cm = 154 cm^2.

Example 2

Find the radius of a circle if the area of the circle is 112 cm^2, given $\pi = 22/7$. Round the number to the nearest whole number.

Solution:

Area of circle = πr^2

112 $cm^2 = 22/7 * r^2$

Multiply by 7 to get rid of the denominator of 22.

$7 * 112\ cm^2 = 7 * 22/7 * r^2$

$784\ cm^2 = 22\ r^2$

Divide through by 22.

$784\ cm^2/22 = 22\ r^2/22$

$35.64\ cm^2 = r^2$

Find the square root of both sides.

$\sqrt{35.64\ cm^2} = \sqrt{r^2}$

5.97 cm = r

Thus, r = 5.97 cm, or 6.0 cm, to the nearest whole number.

Circumference of a Circle

The distance around a circle is its circumference. The circumference of a circle is calculated with circumference = $2\pi r$.

Example 1

Calculate the circumference of a circle of radius 5 cm, given $\pi = 3.142$.

Solution:

Circumference of the circle = $2\pi r$

Circumference of the circle = 2 * 3.142 * 5 cm = 31.42 cm.

Example 2

If the circumference of a circle is 100 cm, calculate its radius if $\pi = 3.142$.

Solution:

Circumference of the circle = 2πr

Given: r = 100 cm, π = 3.142

100 cm = 2 * 3.142 * r

100 cm = 6.284r

Divide through by 6.284

100 cm/6.284 = 6.284r/6.284

15.91 cm = r.

Volume of a Cylinder

The volume of a cylinder of radius r and height h is given by $V = \pi r^2 h$.

Example 1

Calculate the volume of a cylinder to the nearest whole number if the radius and height of the cylinder are 8 cm and 12 cm, respectively. π = 3.142.

Solution:

Radius of the cylinder = 8 cm

Height of the cylinder = 12 cm

Volume of the cylinder = $\pi r^2 h$

Volume of the cylinder = 3.142 * 8 cm * 8 cm * 12 cm

Volume of the cylinder = 2,413.056 cm^3, or 2,413 cm^3 to the nearest whole number.

Example 2

Find the height of a cylinder of volume 1,200 cm^3 if the radius of the cylinder is 10 cm. π = 3.142. Express your answer in one decimal place.

Solution:

Radius of the cylinder = 10 cm

Volume of the cylinder = 1,200 cm^3

Height of the cylinder = x

Volume of a cylinder = $\pi r^2 h$

1,200 cm^3 = 3.142 * 10 cm * 10 cm * h

1,200 cm^3 = 314.2 $cm^2 h$

Divide through by 3.142 cm^2

1,200 cm^3/314.2 cm^2 = 314.2 $cm^2 h$/314.2 cm^2

3.8192 cm = h, or h = 3.8 cm to one decimal place.

Example 3

Find the radius of a cylinder if the volume of the cylinder is 800 cm^3 and it is 12 cm tall.

Solution:

Volume of the cylinder = 800 cm^3

Height of the cylinder = 12 cm

Volume of a cylinder = $\pi r^2 h$

800 cm^3 = 3.142 * 12 cm * r^2

800 cm^3 = 37.704 r^2

Divide both sides by 37.704

800 cm^3/37.704 = 37.704 r^2/37.704

21.22cm = r^2

Find the square root of both sides

$\sqrt{21.22}$ cm = $\sqrt{r^2}$

4.6065 = r, or r = 4.6 cm to one decimal place.

Total Surface Area of a Cylinder

For a cylinder of radius r and height h, the total surface area of the cylinder is total surface area = $2\pi r (r + h)$.

Example 1

Calculate the total surface area of a cylinder with a 5 cm radius, standing 10 cm tall.

Solution:

Radius of the cylinder, r = 5 cm

Height of the cylinder, h = 10 cm

Total surface area of the cylinder = 2πr (r + h)

TSA = 2 * 3.142 * 5 (5 cm + 10 cm)

TSA = 31.42 (15)

TSA = 471.3 cm^2.

Example 2

Given that the total surface area of a cylinder is 1,571 cm^2 and the radius of the cylinder is 15 cm, find its height.

Solution:

Total surface area of the cylinder = 1,571 cm^2

Radius of the cylinder = 15 cm

Height of the cylinder = x

Total surface area of a cylinder = 2πr (r + h)

1,571cm^2 = 2 * 3.142 * 15 cm (h + 15 cm)

1,571cm^2 = 94.26 cm (h + 15 cm)

Divide through by 94.26 cm

1,571cm^2 / 94.26 cm = [94.26 cm (h + 15 cm)]/ 94.26 cm

16.67 cm = h + 15 cm

Organize the like terms.

16.67 cm = 15 cm = h

h = 1.67 cm.

Perimeter of a Trapezoid

Add together all the sides of a trapezoid to calculate its perimeter. Thus, for a trapezoid of sides a, b, c and d, the perimeter is P = a + b + c + d.

Example 1

Calculate the perimeter of a trapezoid with sides 5 cm, 6 cm, 8 cm and 10 cm.

Solution:

Perimeter = sum of all sides

Perimeter of the trapezoid = 5 cm + 6 cm + 8 cm + 10 cm = 29 cm.

Example 2

If three sides of a trapezoid are 8 cm, 11 cm and 12 cm, find the length of the fourth side of the trapezoid if its perimeter is 45 cm.

Solution:

Sides of the trapezoid = 8 cm, 11 cm and 12 cm

Fourth side of the trapezoid = x

Perimeter of a trapezoid = sum of all its sides

Thus, 45 cm = 8 cm + 11 cm + 12 cm +x.

45 cm = 31 cm + x

Organize the like terms.

45 cm – 31 cm = x

14 cm = x.

Area of a Trapezoid

The area of a trapezoid of bases a and b and height h is A = h (a + b)/2 or h/2 (a + b).

Example 1

Find the area of a trapezoid with bases 10 cm and 12 cm if the trapezoid is 15 cm tall.

Solution:

Base a = 10 cm

Base b = 12 cm

Height h = 15 cm

Area of the trapezoid = 15 cm/2 (10 cm + 12 cm)

Area = 7.5 cm (22 cm) = 165 cm^2.

Example 2

If a trapezoid has two bases, 8 cm and 12 cm, respectively, how tall is the trapezoid if its area is 200 cm^2?

Solution:

Base a = 8 cm

Base b = 12 cm

Height h = x

Area = 200 cm^2

Area of a trapezoid = h/2 (a + b)

200 cm^2 = h/2 (8 cm + 12 cm)

200 cm^2 = h/2 (20 cm)

200 cm^2 = 10 cm

Divide through by 10 cm

200 cm^2/10 cm = 10h/10 cm

20 cm = h.

Volume of a Cube

A cube is a three-dimensional object with six faces, 12 edges and eight vertices. The only difference between a cube and a cuboid is that a cube has equal length, width and height on all sides.

The formula for finding the volume of a cube is V = length * width * height. Since all the sides of a cube are equal, the volume can also be calculated by length * length * length or l^3.

Example 1

Calculate the volume of a cube with 15 cm sides.

Solution:

Length of the cube = 15 cm

Volume of a cube = l^3

Volume of the cube = 15^3 = 3,375 cm^3.

Example 2

If the volume of a cube is 1,728 cm^3, find its length.

Solution:

Length of the cube = l

Volume of a cube = l^3

1,728 cm^3 = l^3

Find the cube root of both sides.

$\sqrt[3]{1{,}728\ cm^3} = \sqrt[3]{l^3}$

12 cm = length of the cube.

Volume of a Cuboid

A cuboid is a geometric shape with some vertices at 90 degrees. A cuboid has rectangular faces, and its opposite sides are equal. The area of its four sides, not counting the bottom and top faces, make up its lateral surface area.

The formula for calculating the lateral surface area is A = 2 (l + b) * h, representing the cuboid's length, width and height. Another formula for calculating the area of a cuboid is the perimeter of the base * height.

Example 1

What is the lateral surface area of a cuboid of length 8 cm, height 15 cm and width 20 cm?

Solution:

Length = 8 cm

Width = 20 cm

Height = 15 cm

Lateral surface area of a cuboid, LSA = 2 (l + b) * h

LSA = 2 (8cm + 20cm) * 15 cm

LSA = 30 (28cm) = 840 cm^2.

Example 2

If the lateral surface area of a cuboid 10 cm tall is 400 cm^2, calculate the sum of its length and width.

Solution:

Area = 400 cm^2

Height = 10 cm

Sum of its length and width = l + b

Lateral surface area of a cuboid = 2 (l + b) * h

400 cm^2 = 2 * 10 cm (l + b)

400 cm^2 = 20 cm (l + b)

Divide through by 20 cm

400 cm^2 /20 cm = 20 cm (l + b)/20 cm

20 cm = l + b.

Example 3

The perimeter of the base of a cuboid 20 cm tall is 30 cm. Calculate the lateral surface area of the cuboid.

Solution:

Height = 20 cm

Perimeter = 30 cm

Lateral surface of the cuboid = perimeter of base * height

LSA = 30 cm * 20 cm = 600 cm^2.

Total Surface Area of a Cuboid

To calculate the total surface area of a cuboid, calculate the areas of the cuboid's six sides using the formula below:

Total surface area = 2 [(l × b) + (l × h) + (b × h)] where l, b, and h are the cuboid's length, width, and height, respectively

Example 1

Find the total surface area of a cuboid if the length of the cuboid is 10 cm and its width and height are 8 cm and 12 cm, respectively.

Solution:

Length = 10 cm

Width = 8 cm

Height = 12 cm

Total surface area of a cuboid = 2 [(l × b) + (l × h) + (b × h)]

TSA = 2 [(10 cm × 8 cm) + (10 cm × 12 cm) + (8 cm × 12 cm)]

TSA = 2 [(80 cm^2) + (120 cm^2) + (96 cm^2)]

TSA = 2 (296 cm^2) = 592 cm^2.

Example 2

Calculate the total surface area of a cuboid of length 12 cm, width 20 cm and height 30 cm.

Solution:

Length = 12 cm

Width = 20 cm

Height = 30 cm

Total surface area = 2 [(l × b) + (l × h) + (b × h)]

TSA = 2 [(12 cm × 20 cm) + (10 cm × 30 cm) + (20 cm × 30 cm)]

TSA = 2 [(240 cm^2) + (300 cm^2) + (600 cm^2)]

TSA = 2 (1,140 cm^2) = 2,280 cm^2.

Volume of a Cuboid

The volume of a cuboid is a measure of its base area and height. Hence, it is calculated with the formula V = A * h, where A and h are the cuboid's area and height, respectively.

Example 1

If the base area of a 10 cm tall cuboid is 20 cm^2, calculate its volume.

Solution:

Height = 10 cm

Base = 20 cm^2

Volume = area * height

Volume = 20 cm^2 * 10 cm = 200 cm^3.

Example 2

If the volume of a cuboid is 250 cm^3, find its height if its base area is 15 cm^2.

Solution:

Base = 15 cm^2

Volume = 250 cm^3

Volume = base area * height

250 cm^3 = 15 cm^2 * height

Divide through by 15 cm^2

250 cm^3/15 cm^2 = (15 cm^2 * height)/15 cm^2

16.67 cm = height.

Area of a Rhombus

There are two formulas for finding the area of a rhombus. For a given height and base, the area can be calculated with the formula A = height * base.

Otherwise, if you are given diagonals d1 and d2, you can use the following formula to find the area of the rhombus: (d1 * d2)/2.

Example 1

Find the area of a rhombus if its diagonals are 15 cm and 20 cm, respectively.

Solution:

Diagonal 1, d1 = 15 cm

Diagonal 2, d2 = 20 cm

Area of a rhombus = (d1 * d2)/2

Area of the rhombus = (15 cm * 20 cm)/2

Area = 300 cm^2/2 = 150 cm^2.

Example 2

If a rhombus is 20 cm tall and its base is 25 cm, calculate its area.

Solution:

Base = 25 cm

Height = 20 cm

Area of rhombus = base * height

Area of the given rhombus = 20 cm * 25 cm = 500 cm^2.

Example 3

If the area of a rhombus is 200 cm^2, calculate the second diagonal if one of the diagonals is 10 cm.

Solution:

Area of the rhombus = 200 cm^2

Diagonal 1, d1 = 10 cm

Diagonal 2, d2 = x

Area of a rhombus with diagonals d1 and d2 = (d1 * d2)/2

200 cm^2 = (10 cm * x)/2

200 cm^2 = 5 cmx

Divide through by 5 cm

200 cm^2/5 cm = 5 cmx/5 cm

40 cm = x.

Example 4

If the base of a rhombus with a 150 cm^2 area is 30 cm, how tall is the rhombus?

Solution:

Base of the rhombus = 30 cm

Area of the rhombus = 150 cm^2

Height of the rhombus = x

Area of a rhombus with height h and base b = b * h

150 cm^2 = 30 cm * h

Divide through by 30 cm

150 cm^2/30 cm = (30 cm * h)/30 cm = 5 cm.

Statistics and Probability

Probability is a branch of mathematics dealing with how probable it is that a random event will occur. The probability of the occurrence of an event lies between zero and one. These values mean the event cannot happen and can happen, respectively.

The probability of an event is represented by the formula:

Probability of event happening P (E) = Number of positive outcomes/total number of possible outcomes.

The probability that an event will occur is represented by P (E), and the probability that the event will not occur is represented by P (E'). In a system, P (E) + P (E') = 1.

Example 1

There are 3 red balls, 2 yellow balls and 5 blue balls in a basket. What is the probability of picking a yellow ball from the basket?

Solution:

Number of red balls = 3

Number of yellow balls = 2

Number of blue balls = 5

Total number of balls in the basket = red balls + yellow balls + blue balls

Total number of balls in the basket = 3 balls + 2 balls + 5 balls = 10 balls

Total number of possible outcomes = 10

The probability of picking a yellow ball = number of yellow balls/total number of possible outcomes = 2/10

Simplify the result by dividing by 2.

2/10 = 1/5

Therefore, the probability of picking a yellow ball from the basket is 1/5.

Example 2

If the probability that an event will occur is 1/3, what is the probability that it will not happen?

Solution:

Probability that the event will occur P (E) = 1/3

Probability that it will not occur = P (E') = x

Recall that P (E) + P (E') = 1.

Therefore, 1/3 + x = 1.

Organize the like terms.

x = 1 – 1/3

x = 2/3

Hence, the probability that the event will not occur is 2/3.

Example 3

If Kenny rolls a dice, what is the probability that he will roll a 2?

Solution:

Sample space = {1, 2, 3, 4, 5, 6}

Total number of outcomes = 6

Number of possible outcomes = 1. This is because a dice has only one face with a specific number from 1 to 6.

Therefore, the probability of rolling a 2 is 1/6.

Example 4

If Toby rolls two dice, find the probability that the sum of the two dice equals 6.

Solution:

The possible outcome is:

Outcome = { (1,1), (1,2), (1,3), (1,4), (1,5), (1,6), (2,1), (2,2), (2,3), (2,4), (2,5), (2,6) (3,1), (3,2), (3,3), (3,4), (3,5), (3,6), (4,1), (4,2), (4,3), (4,4), (4,5), (4,6), (5,1), (5,2), (5,3), (5,4), (5,5), (5,6), (6,1), (6,2), (6,3), (6,4), (6,5), (6,6) }

Note, 1,1 means that both dice may give 1 as the outcome; 3,6 shows that the first dice may show 3; while the second displays 6, and so on.

The event of getting the sum of 6 (E) are {(1,5) (2,4), (3,3), (4,2), and (5,1)}.

Number of outcomes (E) = 5

Total number of possible outcomes, S = 36

P (E) = n (E)/n(S) = 5/36

Therefore, the probability of getting the sum of 6 from rolling two dice is 5/36.

Example 5

If Kenny rolls a dice, what is the probability of getting a 2 or 4?

Total number of possible outcomes = 6: {1, 2, 3, 4, 5, and 6}

Total number of favorable outcomes = 2: {2, 4}

The probability of 2 or 4 = 2/6 = 1/3

Thus, the probability of getting a 2 or a 4 from the toss is 1/3.

Tossing a Coin

When a coin is tossed, it will show either heads or tails, H or T. The probability of coming up with either of the two is 1/2. This is because there are two possible outcomes, heads or tails. The number of favorable outcomes is 1 because you cannot get both heads and tails from a single toss. Hence, the number of favorable outcomes/number of possible outcomes = 1/2.

Example 1

Suppose you toss a coin twice. What is the probability of getting at least one tail?

Solution:

The possible outcomes for tossing a coin twice are HH, TH, TT and HT. Thus, the number of possible outcomes is 4.

However, the favorable outcomes with at least one tail are TH, TT and HT. The number of favorable outcomes is 3.

Therefore, the possibility of getting at least one tail = number of favorable outcomes/number of possible outcomes = 3/4.

Hence, the probability of getting at least one tail from tossing a coin twice is 3/4.

Example 2

A man tossed two coins randomly 100 times and found that two heads appeared 40 times, one tail appeared 15 times, one head appeared 20 times and two tails appeared 25 times. If such coins are tossed randomly, what is the probability of getting 2 tails?

Solution:

Number of trials = 100

Number of times that 2 tails appeared = 25

P (getting two tails) = number of times that 2 tails appeared / total number of trials = 25/100, or 1/4

Hence, the probability of getting at least two = 1/4.

Example 3

What is the probability of getting heads or tails in a single toss of a coin?

Solution:

Number of possible outcomes = 2: {H, T}

Number of favorable outcomes = 2: {H,T}

Probability of getting heads or tails = number of favorable outcomes/number of possible outcomes = 2/2 = 1

Thus, the probability of getting heads or tails in a single toss of coin = 1.

Statistics

Statistics is a branch of mathematics primarily concerned with the study of data collection and analysis. It also deals with the interpretation, organization and presentation of data.

In statistics, data can be represented in a number of ways, such as pie charts, bar graphs, dot plots, stem and leaf plots, line graphs and frequency distribution. Other methods of data representation are scatterplots, histograms, cumulative tables, graphs and grouped frequency distribution.

Mean

You can find the mean of two or more numbers by adding the numbers and finding their average.

Example 1

What is the mean of 5 and 9?

Solution:

Step 1: Add the two numbers.

Step 2: Find their average.

To find the mean of 5 and 9, add the numbers and divide by 2.

$= (5 + 9)/2 = 14/2 = 7.$

Example 2

Find the mean of 9, 2, 5, 8 and 10.

Solution:

There are five numbers in the list. The mean is the sum of the numbers divided by the number of elements in the list.

Sum of the numbers: $9 + 2 + 5 + 8 + 10 = 34$

Total number of elements = 5

Mean = sum of numbers/total number of elements = 34/5

$34/5 = 6.8.$

Example 3

Find the value of x if 3 + 10 + 7 + 4 + x = 35.

Solution:

Total number of elements = 5

Sum of the elements = 3 + 10 + 7 + 4 + x

However, the sum of the elements = 35. Thus 3 + 10 + 7 + 4 + x = 35.

24 + x = 35

Organize the like terms.

x = 35 – 24 = 11

You can also find the mean of a set of numbers on a frequency table. Consider some examples.

Example 1

Score	Frequency
1	3
2	5
3	2
4	4
5	2

The total number of elements or sum of frequencies = 3 + 5 + 2 + 4 + 2 = 16.

Sum of numbers = (3 * 1) + (2 * 5) + (3 * 2) + (4 * 4) + (5 * 2)

Sum of numbers = 3 + 10 + 6 + 16 + 10 = 45

Mean = sum of numbers/total number of elements

Mean = 45/16 = 2.81.

Example 2

Find the mean score of the soccer players represented in the frequency table below to the nearest whole number.

Player	Number of Goals
Messi	30
Ronaldo	35
Lewandoski	32
Immobile	40
Mbappe	34

This example is a bit different from the preceding example.

Number of players = 5

Total number of goals = 30 + 35 + 32 + 40 + 34

Mean = total number of goals/number of players

Mean = 171/5 = 34.2, or 34.0 to the nearest whole number.

Mode

The mode refers to the number with the largest appearance in a list of numbers. To find the mode, rearrange the numbers in ascending or descending order to find the number that appears most often.

Example 1

What is the mode of these numbers: 2, 6, 8, 2, 5, 8, 2, 5, 2, 9?

Solution:

Rearrange the numbers in ascending order.

Therefore, 2, 6, 8, 2, 5, 8, 2, 5, 2, 9 = 2, 2, 2, 5, 5, 6, 8, 8, 9 when rearranged.

As you can see, 2 appears three times, 6 appears once, 8 appears twice and 9 appears only once. From the list, 2 appears the most times.

Thus, 2 is the mode.

Example 2

Find the mode of 4, 6, 2, 7, 3, 8, 9, 7, 3, 7.

Solution:

Rearrange the numbers.

4, 6, 2, 7, 3, 8, 9, 7, 3, 7 = 2, 3, 3, 4, 6, 7, 7, 7, 8, 9

Since 7 appears most in the list, 7 is the mode.

Sometimes there may be more than one mode in a list. You can have bimodal or multimodal numbers with two or more than two modes, respectively.

Example 3

Find the mode of 2, 3, 3, 4, 6, 7, 7, 7, 8, 9, 9 1, 9.

Solution:

Rearrange the numbers in ascending order.

2, 3, 3, 4, 6, 7, 7, 7, 8, 9, 9 1, 9 = 1, 2, 3, 3, 4, 6, 7, 7, 7, 8, 9, 9, 9 when rearranged.

From the rearranged numbers, only 7 and 9 appear the same number of times: 3. That is the highest number of appearances. Thus, the mode for the list is 7 and 9. This is a typical example of a bimodal number.

Example 4

Find the mode of the numbers below:

Number	Frequency
2	5
3	4
5	8
7	2
10	1

From the frequency table, 5 is the number that appears the most (8 times). Thus it is the mode.

Median

The median of a set of numbers is the number that appears in the middle of the set when arranged in ascending or descending order.

Example 1

Find the median of this set of numbers: 1, 2, 3, 3, 4, 6, 7, 7, 7, 8, 9, 9, 9.

Solution:

Rearrange the numbers.

2, 3, 3, 4, 6, 7, 7, 7, 8, 9, 9 1, 9 = 1, 2, 3, 3, 4, 6, 7, 7, 7, 8, 9, 9, 9 when rearranged.

To find the median, use the formula (n + 1)/2.

Here, n is the number of elements in the list = 13.

Thus the median is (13 + 1)/2 = 14/2 = 7.

Example 2

Find the median: 2, 6, 1, 7, 2, 8, 9, 3, 7, 5, 3, 4, 9, 2, 6.

Solution:

n = 15

Median = (n + 1)/2

(15+ 1)/2 = 16/2 = 8

Hence, the eighth number is the median.

Rearrange the numbers.

1, 2, 2, 2, 3, 3, 4, 5, 6, 6, 7, 7, 8, 9, 9

The eighth number is 5. Hence, 5 is the median.

Chapter Three: Writing

As a teacher, your job description is not limited to reading and teaching. Sometimes, you may have to do some writing too. You may have to write for an audience, to the school board or to some agencies as circumstances demand. This is in addition to the positive impact that writing will have on you as a teacher, so you must understand the necessary skills that will boost your writing abilities.

In this section we will focus on sentence construction, error identification, parts of speech and research skills.

Sentence Structure

Sentence structure refers to the grammatical arrangement of a sentence. This focuses on the arrangement of the subjects, verbs and other elements of your writing. Let's consider the types of sentences and their components.

Types of Sentences

There are four types of sentences: simple sentences, compound sentences, complex sentences and compound-complex sentences. Each of these sentence types is defined by its unique elements.

Simple Sentences

As the name implies, this is the simplest form of sentence structure. A simple sentence contains an independent clause. This is a clause that is made up of just two components: a subject and a verb. Nevertheless, an independent clause is not considered a simple sentence if it does not convey a complete thought. So, a meaningless independent clause does not qualify as a simple sentence.

Some examples of simple sentences include:

- I am going home.
- I am tired.
- She lost her purse.

Compound Sentences

A complex sentence consists of two or more independent clauses. These clauses are joined by a conjunction to make them a compound sentence.

Each of the independent clauses can convey a complete thought without the other clause.

Consider the following example:

- I am going home because I am hungry.

This compound sentence contains two independent clauses: “I am going home” and “I am hungry.” Remove the conjunctions and what you have are two simple sentences.

Some other examples of compound sentences include:

- I hit the ball and it hit the car.
- I ran so fast because I was late for the exam.

Complex Sentences

Another sentence structure is the complex sentence. It is made of two types of clauses: an independent clause and one or two dependent clauses. While the independent clause can stand alone and convey a meaningful message, a dependent clause *cannot* stand alone and depends on other clauses for existence.

A complex sentence starts with a subordinating conjunction or a relative pronoun. That is the major difference between this class of clause and its independent counterpart. Consider the two examples below:

- She left in a hurry after submitting her assignment.

“She left in a hurry” is an independent clause, while “after submitting her assignment” is the dependent clause.

- The place is always flooded after a heavy rainfall.

“The place is always flooded” is an independent clause, while “after a heavy rainfall” is a dependent clause.

A dependent clause is otherwise known as a subordinate clause.

Compound-Complex Sentences

As you can see from the name, this is a hybrid sentence that combines the attributes of a compound sentence and a complex sentence. Compound-complex sentences contain at least one subordinate clause and at least two independent clauses.

Consider the following example:

- I would have bought the book when I saw it in the bookstore, but I was dead broke.

Sentence Construction Tips

- There are two types of articles in English: definite and indefinite. When referring to specific nouns, the definite article is used. Indefinite articles are used for general nouns. While *a* and *an* are examples of indefinite articles, *the* is the definite article.
- When writing, pay attention to your subject and the corresponding noun. Do they align or not? If you use the wrong sentence and verb, there will not be agreement between them, and that will automatically cause a grammatical error. Subject and verb agreement is discussed extensively later. You will learn the basic rules that guide the agreement between these two elements of a sentence.
- You must be familiar with punctuation marks and know the appropriate ones to use. These will also be discussed in detail later in this chapter.
- The most popular sentence construction starts with subject, verb, object, provided that an object is needed in the sentence.

Consider the following example:

- The boy kicked the ball.

In this sentence, *the boy* is the subject. The verb is *kicked* while *the ball* is the object. That is the right order.

What happens if the order of arrangement is changed? Let's see.

- The ball is kicked by the boy.

Here, the object comes first, followed by the verb and, finally, the subject. While this may be a correct passive tense, many English experts and critics frown on this order.

- Sentence length deserves attention too. You do not want to cultivate the habit of writing only short or long sentences. If you are accustomed to the former, your writing will be stilted and difficult to read fluently. On the other hand, sentences that are too long may be difficult to read, as readers may get lost. Vary your sentence lengths.
- Learn to logically connect one point to another to make your writing flow well and help your audience better understand the main ideas. You can connect points in your passages with words such as *similarly*, *in addition*, *also*, *furthermore*, *moreover* and *likewise* when indicating similarity. To draw contrast between two ideas, use contrasting words and phrases such as *on the other hand*, *nevertheless*, *conversely*, *but*, *in contrast*, *alternatively* and *yet*.

Sentence Construction Errors and How to Avoid Them

A part of good writing is knowing what to write; arranging it in a logical order is also important. While the former gives you something to write about, the latter makes your writing of interest to your target audience.

Many writers make common sentence construction errors. Your ability to identify sentence fragments, comma splices and run-ons while editing your writing will help you to present a clearer picture to your readers, better conveying your message.

Sentence Fragments: A fragment consists of a subject without a predicate. Fragments are commonly referred to as incomplete sentences.

Consider this sentence:

- Confusing and difficult to read.

This sentence is obviously incomplete. The question it raises is, what is confusing and difficult to read? Until the sentence provides a satisfying answer to that question, you have a sentence fragment.

On the other hand, "The legal book is confusing and difficult to read" is complete. It answers the question we previously asked. What is difficult to read? The legal book. As a good writer, you must avoid such mistakes. Ensure that all the sentences are complete and meaningful.

Comma Splices: This error occurs when two independent clauses are joined by a comma that is not grammatically correct. Comma splices obscure the relationship between the ideas in your writing.

An effective strategy for correcting this error is to use the appropriate punctuation mark. If the sentence contains two independent clauses, a semicolon is appropriate to use.

Consider the following example:

- She is down with the flu, she can't go to work today.

Splitting the sentence into two with a semicolon, you have: "She is down with the flu; she can't go to work today." Note that this rule applies to two independent clauses only.

You may also divide the sentence into smaller sentences and replace the comma with the appropriate punctuation mark.

Consider the following example:

- She wanted to go out and because she was sick, she needed help.

The comma in this sentence is misplaced, making the sentence's meaning muddled. Breaking the sentence into two, you have: "She wanted to go out. Because she was sick, she needed help."

You can also use a coordinating conjunction to correct comma splice errors:

Consider the following example:

- She wanted to go out, she ended up watching her favorite TV show.

A coordinating conjunction resolves this error: "She wanted to go out, but she ended up watching her favorite TV show."

Run-Ons: A run-on occurs when two or more independent clauses are merged into a single sentence without the proper punctuation.

Consider the following example:

- They slept very late they didn't wake up on time.

In the sentence, two independent clauses are merged together as one without the appropriate punctuation mark. This makes the sentence difficult to read.

Run-ons can be fixed with the same techniques used for correcting sentence fragments. If there are two independent clauses in the sentence, separate them into two different sentences.

Consider this example:

- They did not come home immediately they were busy playing soccer.

Splitting this sentence into two independent sentences, you have: "They did not come home immediately. They were busy playing soccer." This is much clearer.

Consider the following example:

- They did not come home immediately they were busy playing soccer.

By replacing the comma with a semicolon, we have: "They did not come home immediately; they were busy playing soccer."

The Role of Editing in Writing

Editing your writing helps minimize errors and improve your content. No matter how great your first draft seems, you can always improve it significantly by editing.

While editing a piece of writing, go through your ideas again and cut out irrelevant information, add other important information, rearrange your content as needed for clarity, etc. Also check your punctuation, grammar and sentence structure.

To edit your work better, consider these useful tips:

Take a break from writing before you commence editing. This enables you to look at the work objectively and identify errors more easily than if you've been staring at the same page for hours on end.

Put yourself in your readers' shoes. With that mindset, go through the article again and consider the following questions:

- Are you satisfied with the piece or not?
- Does it convey your desired message?
- Did you use the right words to convey your ideas?
- Is your syntax and sentence structure correct?

As you answer these questions, among others, you will have a broad idea of necessary adjustments that need to be made to the piece to improve its quality.

You may also break the editing process into multiple rounds. In the first round, focus on content. Next, focus on organization. Finally, focus on punctuation, grammar, etc. By concentrating on one type of issue at a time, you are able to do a more thorough job than you would if you were to attempt to fix all the issues at once.

Ask a friend. If you have a trusted friend or any other reliable person, let them go through your work. They may identify issues you have accidentally overlooked.

Parts of Speech

There are eight parts of speech in English: nouns, pronouns, adjectives, prepositions, verbs, adverbs, interjections and conjunctions.

Nouns

A noun is a person, animal, place or thing. Thus, *dog*, *Canada*, *book*, *pen*, *Felix* and *computer* are examples of nouns.

There are different types of nouns. These are:

Common Nouns: This refers to a noun used for naming a group of objects or items. Some examples are *animals*, *vehicles* and *newspapers*.

Proper Nouns: Proper nouns identify single, specific entities. Some examples are *Jessica, Kansas, Toyota* and *New York Post*.

Abstract Nouns: Abstract nouns are not visible to the physical eye. They can be felt and experienced, though. Emotions, traits and concepts are examples of abstract nouns. The list includes *love, intelligence* and *freedom*.

Concrete Nouns: While you cannot see abstract nouns physically, you *can* see and touch concrete nouns. Examples include *bus, house, dog, person* and *horseshoe*.

Concrete nouns can be countable or uncountable.

Collective Nouns: These refer to a group of objects or people. Examples are *flock, team, board, crowd, bouquet, forest, choir, pair, fleet* and more.

Pronouns

Pronouns are words or phrases used as replacements for nouns in sentences. Examples of common pronouns are *he, she, it, they, them* and *we*. For instance, "Tony is a handsome man" can be rewritten as "He is a handsome man," replacing the name or noun *Tony* with the pronoun *he*.

Consider the following example:

- Tina and Kelly are friends.

If you rewrite the sentence using a pronoun, you get: "They are friends." The pronoun *they* has been used to replace the nouns *Tina* and *Kelly*.

There are different types of pronouns:

Personal Pronouns: Personal pronouns are used to replace people's names. As such, they can act as the objects or subjects of a sentence. *She, her, us, him* and *them* are typical examples of personal pronouns.

Indefinite Pronouns: Indefinite pronouns refer to nonspecific nouns. Examples include *whoever, somebody, anybody, someone* and *nobody*.

Consider the following example:

- Tell everyone to attend the lecture.

Here, *everyone* refers to no one in particular, although it is directed to a group of people.

Demonstrative Pronouns: Demonstrative pronouns replace nouns. Sometimes, when such pronouns perform the roles of demonstrative adjectives, they modify nouns or pronouns. Common examples of demonstrative pronoun are *that, those, these* and *this.*

Relative Pronouns: Relative pronouns are used to connect a phrase or a clause to a pronoun or a noun.

Possessive Pronouns: Possessive pronouns are used to express ownership or possession. *Their*, *your*, *mine* and *ours* are typical examples of this type of pronoun.

Intensive Pronouns: Intensive pronouns come after the pronoun or noun that they intensify or emphasize in a sentence.

Prepositions

Prepositions connect nouns, phrases or pronouns to another phrase or pronoun. Although prepositions sometimes precede gerund verbs, they usually precede a noun.

There are many types of prepositions:

Prepositions of Time: Prepositions of time indicate when something will definitely occur. They can also indicate the actual time something occurred in the past or when it currently occurs.

Some examples are:

- He got home from work around 9:30 p.m.
- Debra arrived at her destination 15 minutes early.

Prepositions of Agent: The causal relationships between verbs and nouns are expressed with preposition of agent. Two examples of these prepositions are *with* and *by*.

Some examples are:

- The little girl is playing with her doll.
- The goal was scored by one of the best footballers in the world.

Prepositions of Direction: Prepositions of direction, such as *through*, *toward*, *to* and *into,* specify the subject's direction.

Some examples are:

- I will pass through the subway tunnel on my way home.
- The animal walked into the trap.

Prepositions of Instrument: Prepositions of instrument are used for an array of instruments, devices or machines. Examples of such prepositions are *with, by* and *on*.

Some examples are:

- I will go by the house.
- He opened the lock with the key.

Prepositions of Place: This type of preposition addresses the specific location of a person, object, or item. Three common examples of prepositions of place are *on*, *in* and *at*.

In is used to define a virtual or physical boundary.

An example is:

- She is in the shopping mall.

When defining the relationship between two objects or things in relation to their surfaces, *on* is used.

An example is:

- The cell phone is on the table.

At is a preposition of place used for defining specific places.

An example is:

- She is at home.

Verbs

A verb is an action word. It describes the subject's action in a given sentence. A sentence is incomplete without a verb.

An action verb can be intransitive or transitive. Action verbs that are incomplete without a direct object to receive the action the subject performs are transitive verbs. They require an object or a recipient of the subject's action.

An example of an action verb is:

- I am watching my favorite TV show.

The action verb is *watching*. The object is *my favorite TV show*.

On the other hand, intransitive verbs do not require an object. They express complete thoughts without depending on a third party to make them complete. Examples of transitive verbs include *sings, plays, dances.*

Auxiliary Verbs: These verbs express concepts such as modality and emphasis. When they appear in any sentence, they add to the sentence's functional or grammatical meaning by showing the verb's tense or time. Auxiliary verbs are also referred to as helping verbs because of their role in a sentence. *May, have, need, has, will, had* and *should* are a few examples of auxiliary verbs.

Regular Verbs: Regular verbs form their tenses by following an established pattern. Many verbs form their past tense or past participles by adding *-d* or *-ed* as a suffix. Most verbs that end in *-y* follow a different pattern for their past and past participle tenses. The *-y* must be changed to *i* with *ed* added to make its past tense and past participle. Some examples of such verbs are *bury, create* and *learn.*

Irregular Verbs: These verbs do not follow a regular pattern when forming their past tense and past participle. Some examples are *sit, go* and *drink.*

Adverbs

Adverbs describe or modify another adverb, adjective, verb or a group of words. They are also extensively used to modify clauses, sentences, determiners and prepositions.

The following are adverb types:

Adverbs of Manner: Adverbs of manner describe the manner in which someone does something or how something happens. These adverbs end in *-ly*. *Quickly, arrogantly, beautifully, slowly* and *suddenly* are some examples.

Adverbs of Time: While adverbs of manner focus on the way an action occurs, adverbs of time place emphasis on the time of the action. These adverbs answer the question, "When?"

The location of the adverb in a sentence determines the urgency of the time information provided by the adverb. The adverb will start the sentence if the time is very important. Otherwise, it concludes a sentence. *Always, recently, sometimes* and *soon* are some examples.

Adverbs of Degree: These adjectives express intensity. They modify the adjective, noun or adverb they precede in a sentence.

Adverbs of Place: Adverbs of place are used when the goal is to provide background information about the location of an action. They mostly are placed after the main object or verb to provide additional information about the location. Some examples are *below, above, outside, here* and *everywhere*.

Adverbs of Frequency: Adverbs of frequency express the frequency of the occurrence of an action. You can find adverbs of frequency before a sentence's main verb. Examples include *always, sometimes, seldom* and *rarely*.

Interjections

Sudden emotions and strong feelings are expressed with interjections. A writer may use this part of speech to introduce emotion into a piece. Some strong emotions that can be expressed with interjections are *happiness, sadness, shock* and *excitement*.

Examples of interjectional statements include:

- Oh my God!
- What a miss!
- Ouch!
- No way!

Conjunctions

Conjunctions are words that connect multiple words, clauses or phrases.

Conjunctions are classified into four types:

Subordinating Conjunctions: When two clauses have different grammatical values, they are connected with subordinating conjunctions such as *so that, unless, until, since, although, when, how, after* and others. They are especially useful for connecting independent and dependent clauses.

Coordinating Conjunctions: Sentences that are grammatically similar are connected with coordinating conjunctions. Examples of this type of conjunction *but not limited to, with, but, for, or* and *nor*.

Adverbial Conjunctions: Adverbial conjunctions join independent clauses. Otherwise known as conjunctive adverbs, adverbial conjunctions are usually followed by a comma and preceded with a semicolon. Some examples are *consequently, in contrast, however, likewise* and *accordingly*.

Correlative Conjunctions: Correlative conjunctions show a contrast or comparison between ideas or words. Examples include *not only, but also, either* and *neither*.

Examples of correlative conjunctions used in sentences include:

- The boy is not only brilliant but ambitious.
- She is neither a fool nor a criminal.

Adjectives

Adjectives are noun modifiers. While modifying a noun, an adjective furnishes the reader with more attributes of the noun under consideration. Some attributes of a noun that can be described by an adjective are its *appearance, size* and *shape.*

Long, old, expensive and *beautiful* are some common examples of adjectives.

The following are the types of adjectives:

Interrogative Adjectives: These adjectives are used for asking questions. *What, which* and *whose* are examples.

Examples include:

- What are you doing there?
- Whose book is this?

Demonstrative Adjectives: Demonstrative adjectives demonstrate or indicate nouns. *Those, these, that* and *this* are commonly used demonstrative adjectives.

Indefinite Adjectives: Indefinite adjectives function as indefinite nouns. They are used to describe nonspecific nouns. Some indefinite adjectives are *any, few* and *many.*

Possessive Adjectives: Possession is expressed with possessive adjectives. Thus, these adjectives share some similarities with possessive pronouns. *His, theirs, mine* and *hers* are some possessive adjectives.

Examples include:

- The book is hers.
- The toy is his.

Number Adjectives: A number adjective helps readers find more information about the quantity of an object in a sentence. For instance, consider the following example:

- There are 30 boys on the school bus.

Here, *30* is the number adjective that helps the reader know the specific number of the object, *students,* in the sentence. The number answers the question, How many boys are on the school bus?

Errors in Parts of Speech and How to Avoid Them

The following are common parts of speech errors.

Adverb Usage: Some common mistakes include placing an adverb before a verb in a sentence. This is often wrong because an adverb should be used after the verb.

Consider some examples:

- She angrily left after the argument.

The correct expression is "She left angrily after the argument."

- The storm furiously swept everything in its path away.

This should read, "The storm swept everything in the path away furiously."

Enough Usage: *Enough* is an adverb that is commonly misapplied too. The error occurs when this adverb is used before the adverb or adjective it is supposed to modify. Consider the following example:

- The piece of land is enough spacious for the project.

This should read, "The piece of land is spacious enough for the project."

Noun-Noun Agreement Error: This is a noun-noun equivalent of the pronoun-noun issue previously addressed. When a noun is used to refer to another noun, the referenced noun must agree with the first noun.

Consider the following example:

- Dele and Kenny are footballer.

The subject in this case is *Dele and Kenny*. Thus, the referenced noun must be plural because they are two people. Hence, the correct expression is "Dele and Kenny are footballers."

Coordinating Conjunctions Usage Errors: A common error associated with coordinating conjunctions is joining two independent clauses without using a comma before the conjunction. The rule indicates that you must precede the coordinating conjunction with a comma. The only exception to this rule is that if the two independent conjunctions to be joined are very short, a comma is not required before the conjunction. Also, if two complements, two verbs, two objects or two subjects are joined with a conjunction, a comma is not needed between them.

Correlative Conjunction Usage Error: A correlative conjunction error arises when a writer mixes up the appropriate correlative conjunction. *Neither* should be completed with *nor*, while *either* requires *or*.

Idiomatic Expression Errors: This error occurs when someone does not use the correct idiomatic expression. For instance, some may be confused whether the right expression is the *lion share* or the *lion's share*.

Frequently Confused Words: Frequently confused words are similar in spellings and pronunciation and are thus mixed up in writing. Consider the following homophones:

- *ascent/assent*
- *a lot/a lot*
- *affect/effect*
- *illusion/allusion*
- *altogether/all together*
- *principal/principle*

Dangling Modifiers: This error occurs when a clause or phrase is not logically or clearly related to the group of words it modifies. Consider this example:

- The small.

The identifier is "small," but it doesn't provide any information about the noun it modifies. A full sentence would be, "The small boy is here."

Parallel Structure Error: The rule of parallel structure stipulates that phrases or words in a series should maintain the same form. Consider the following examples:

- She likes hunting, running and to hike.

This sentence has a parallel structure error. The verbs in the sentence are *hunting*, *running* and *hike*. While the first two are continuous verbs, the third is a present-tense verb. That breaks the rule. To correct this error, all the verbs should be in the present form.

Thus, the correct form is "She likes hunting, running and hiking," or "She likes to hunt, run and hike."

- Hitting your goals in life is neither easy nor is it cheap.

The sentence should read: "Hitting your goals in life is neither easy nor cheap."

Redundancy: Redundancy errors occur when two similar words are used to express the same idea in a sentence. Examples of such words include:

- *absolutely certain*
- *added bonus*
- *at the present time*
- *close proximity*.

Pronoun-Antecedent Agreement Error: This error occurs when there is no agreement between a pronoun and its antecedent. The antecedent of a pronoun is the specific noun the pronoun replaces in a text. Thus, the pronoun and the replaced noun must agree.

For instance, the right pronoun for a female is *she,* while a male requires *he* as the pronoun. Animals and inanimate objects use *it,* while *they* can replace a group of things, animals or people.

Consider this sentence:

- Michael is a great footballer. She is a great athlete.

Generally, Michael is a male name. Thus, the right replacement is the pronoun *he.*

Subject-Verb Agreement Error: Subject-verb agreement errors are a common mistake. Writers often are confused about the most appropriate way to combine a subject and a verb in a sentence.

However, there are two simple rules: If the subject is plural, the verb should be plural. If the subject is singular, the verb should be singular too.

Plural subjects end with *s,* while plural verbs do not end with *s.* Examples of plural subjects are *boys, tables, books, houses* and more, while examples of plural verbs are *go, come, play, dance, walk* and so on.

Most singular subjects do not end with *s.* Examples of singular nouns are *boy, table, book, house. Goes, comes, plays, dances* and *walks* are a few examples of singular verbs. Some exceptions to the rule include *canvas, thesis,* etc.

Noun/Adjective Error: A common error is the confusion about which comes first, the noun or adjective? To avoid this error, note that the qualifying adjective comes before the noun phrase or noun it qualifies.

Consider the following example:

- She is a girl beautiful.

This is wrong because the noun comes before the adjective. The right expression is "She is a beautiful girl."

Punctuation and Capitalization

Capitalization and punctuation are crucial to error-free writing.

Capitalization

Capitalization refers to starting a word with a capital letter. It follows specific rules:

- The first word of a sentence should be capitalized.
- The titles of articles, books or works of art are capitalized. There are some exceptions, though. Conjunctions and short prepositions in titles are not capitalized.
- Capitalize proper nouns such as cities, people's names and brands. i.e., Bob, New York, Rolex.
- When someone's title precedes their name, capitalize the title. i.e., Dr. Jones, not dr. Jones.
- When a title is used as a direct address, capitalize the title. For example, "When will you help me, Mother?"
- Capitalize the letter *i* when it is used independently of other words in a sentence. Its contraction forms should be capitalized too. Two examples are "I am going home after the lecture" and "I'm not aware of the current situation of the company."
- The only condition for capitalizing the points of the compass is when they are used to make reference to specific regions. i.e., "My friend is visiting from the South" versus "I am driving toward the south."

Punctuation

The following are common punctuation marks in the English language:

Periods (.)

The period signifies the end of a sentence that is not an exclamation or a question. This punctuation mark is also used to abbreviate words.

Exclamation Points (!)

An exclamation point expresses strong emotions and feelings.

Question Marks (?)

This punctuation mark is used at the end of an interrogative sentence. Note that when you end a sentence with a question mark, you do not need a period.

Commas (,)

A comma separates a list of objects or items in a sentence.

Consider the following example:

- This guide is divided into three sections. These are mathematics, reading and writing.

The comma also separates independent clauses when such clauses are connected with *but, nor* and *for,* or any other coordinating conjunction.

Consider the following example:

- He wanted to go home, but it was raining.

This is an example of comma-separated independent clauses.

Apostrophes (')

Apostrophes show possession. Consider the following examples:

- This is Tunde's book.
- Our mothers' cars look alike.

Contractions also use an apostrophe. *Should not* becomes *shouldn't, does not* becomes *doesn't* and so on.

Quotation Marks (" " or ' ')

Quotation marks quote words in a sentence. Consider the following example:

- Her mother told her, "It is too cold outside."

The quotation marks reference the mother's advice.

Punctuation Errors and How to Avoid Them

Here are some common punctuation errors and some tips to help you avoid them.

Commas

One common comma error is separating two verb phrases or verbs with a comma. This is wrong because such verbs or phrases should not be separated at all.

Consider the following example:

- I bought, and drove my first car yesterday.

This is wrong. The correct sentence is, “I bought and drove my first car yesterday.” The comma is needless.

When a conjunction joins two noun phrases, two nouns or two noun clauses, they should not be separated with a comma.

Consider the following example:

- My fiancée, and my sister both sent birthday gifts.

This is wrong. “Fiancée” and “sister” are nouns joined by *and*.

The correct sentence is “My fiancée and my sister both sent birthday gifts.”

Apostrophes

A common apostrophe error is an extraneous apostrophe.

Consider some examples:

- There are five ball’s in the basket.
- She has been working for 10 consecutive day’s.

If you remember that apostrophes indicate possession, you will realize why these sentences are wrong.

Mathematics Test 1: Questions

(1) What are whole numbers?

(A) Numbers that are divisible by 2

(B) Countable numbers

(C) Numbers with special attributes

(D) Numbers that are not divisible

(2) Which of the following is true about whole numbers?

(A) They are positive and negative numbers.

(B) They are negative numbers only.

(C) They are positive numbers only.

(D) They are undefined.

(3) What are integers?

(A) Positive and fractional numbers

(B) Positive and negative numbers

(C) Numbers divisible by 2 and 3

(D) Special numbers between 2 and 100

(4) Which of the following is not a complete set of integers?

(A) 12, 36, 79 and 10

(B) 14, 56, 29 and 14

(C) -2/9, 76, 23 and 18

(D) All of the above

(5) Find the sum of 136, 29 and 345.

(A) 610

(B) 510

(C) 600

(D) 500

(6) Add 123 and 73.

(A) 853

(B) 753

(C) 196

(D) 186

(7) What is the first step when adding integers?

(A) Check whether the question is correct.

(B) Check whether the numbers are multiples of 5.

(C) Reorganize the numbers in ascending order.

(D) Reorganize the numbers to ensure their alignment.

(8) A student wants to add a set of integers. Where should the student start?

(A) From the left-hand side

(B) From the right-hand side

(C) From any side

(D) According to the number of elements in the list

(9) What is the first thing to consider when adding integers?

(A) The location of the second integer

(B) The smaller and larger integers

(C) The order of arrangement

(D) The ease or difficulty of the operation

(10) Subtract 57 from 189.

(A) 133

(B) 132

(C) -133

(D) -132

(11) When is it necessary to borrow when subtracting integers?

(A) When the denominator is bigger than the numerator

(B) When one of the numbers is a multiple of 5 and the other is a multiple of 4

(C) When both numbers are multiples of 2 and 4

(D) When the number to be subtracted is smaller than the number it is being subtracted from

(12) What is the difference between adding and subtracting integers versus dividing them?

(A) Addition and subtraction of integers start from the right, while division starts from the left

(B) Addition and subtraction of integers start from the left, while division starts from the right

(C) Addition and subtraction of integers start from the right, while division can start from anywhere

(D) Addition and subtraction of integers start from the left, while division can start from anywhere

(13) Divide 505 by 5.

(A) 155

(B) 11

(C) 55

(D) 101

(14) What happens if the divisor cannot divide the first number in the denominator?

(A) The calculation cannot be performed.

(B) Move to the next three numbers in the numerator.

(C) Move to the next two numbers in the denominator.

(D) Combine the next number in the numerator with it.

(15) Multiply 45 by 15.

(A) 60

(B) 15

(C) 675

(D) 765

(16) Where do you start multiplication of integers?

(A) From the right

(B) From the left

(C) From the middle

(D) From anywhere

(17) What are decimal numbers?

(A) Numbers that are divisible by 2 and 4

(B) Numbers that cannot be directly divided by even numbers

(C) Numbers with a whole and a fractional part

(D) Numbers with a whole and an indivisible part

(18) What do we call the number before the decimal point?

(A) Fractional part

(B) Whole number

(C) Decimal prefix

(D) Decimal suffix

(19) Which of the following operations cannot be performed on decimal numbers?

(A) Addition and subtraction

(B) Division and multiplication

(C) None of the above

(D) A and B

(20) Add 12.34 and 36.79.

(A) 49.12

(B) 49.13

(C) 50.24

(D) 54.23

(21) What should be your primary objective while rearranging decimal numbers during mathematical operations?

(A) Equality of numbers

(B) Alignment of numbers

(C) Simplicity of numbers

(D) Order of operations

(22) Why is zero added to some decimal numbers during mathematical operations?

(A) To increase the number's value

(B) To make the number more appealing

(C) To ensure proper alignment of the numbers

(D) For complex calculations

(23) What is the difference between 252.12 and 875.89?

(A) 623.7

(B) 623.78

(C) 623.77

(D) 623.76

(24) Subtract 34.12 from 123.34.

(A) 89.33

(B) 89.24

(C) 89.22

(D) 87.12

(25) Divide 78.24 by 4.

(A) 19.90

(B) 18.76

(C) 19.26

(D) 19.56

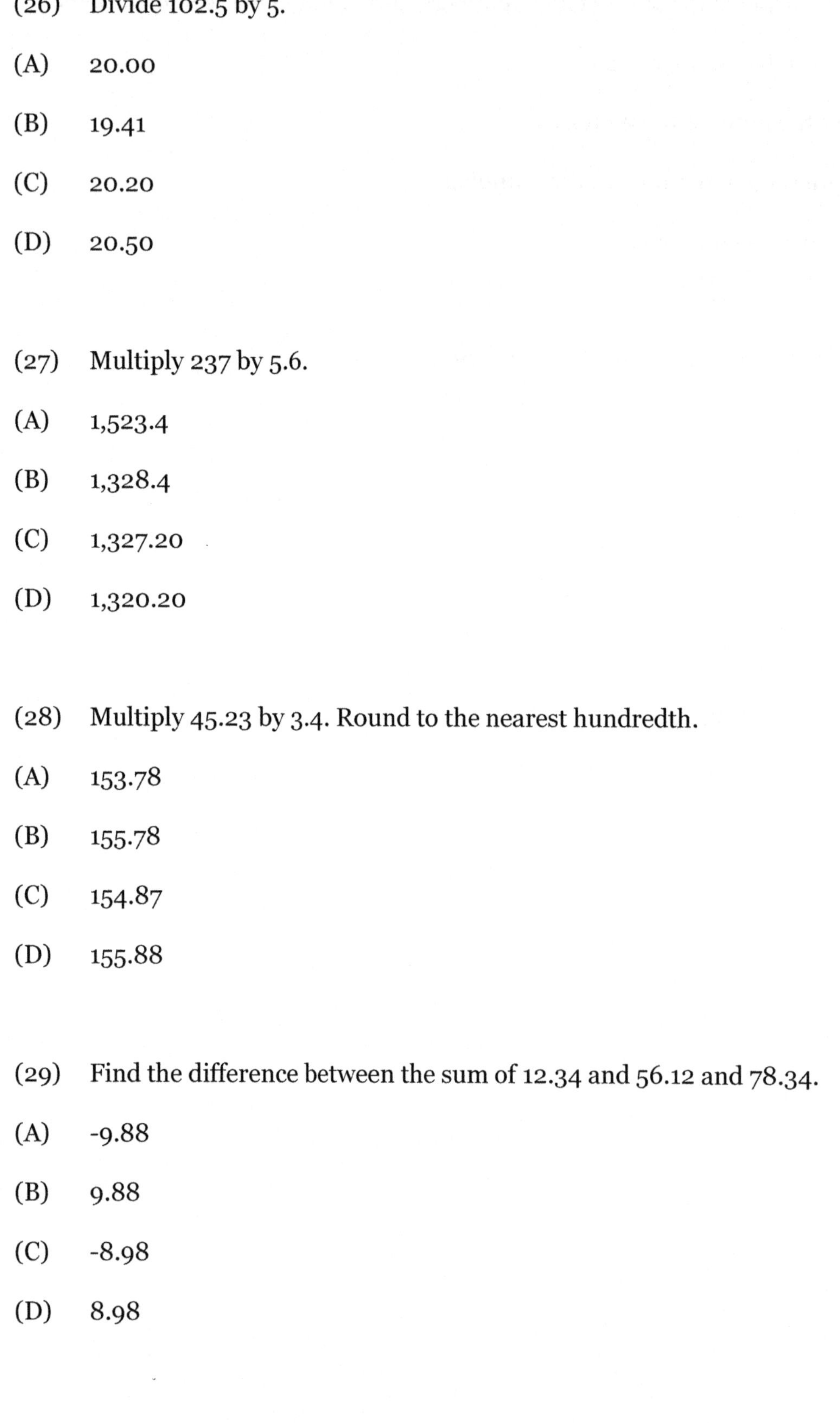

(26) Divide 102.5 by 5.

(A) 20.00

(B) 19.41

(C) 20.20

(D) 20.50

(27) Multiply 237 by 5.6.

(A) 1,523.4

(B) 1,328.4

(C) 1,327.20

(D) 1,320.20

(28) Multiply 45.23 by 3.4. Round to the nearest hundredth.

(A) 153.78

(B) 155.78

(C) 154.87

(D) 155.88

(29) Find the difference between the sum of 12.34 and 56.12 and 78.34.

(A) -9.88

(B) 9.88

(C) -8.98

(D) 8.98

(30) Convert 0.7 to a fraction.

(A) 4/5

(B) 7/10

(C) 3.5/8

(D) 8/9

(31) What is the result of the conversion of 0.8 to a fraction, reduced to simplest terms?

(A) 4/5

(B) 8/9

(C) 3/4

(D) 5/7

(32) Convert 0.6 to a fraction in simplest terms.

(A) 6/10

(B) 4/5

(C) 3/5

(D) 10/12

(33) Which of the following are not types of fractions?

(A) Proper and improper fractions

(B) Improper and mixed fractions

(C) Simple and complex fractions

(D) None of the above

(34) In which of the following is the numerator bigger than the denominator?

(A) Complex fractions

(B) Simple fractions

(C) Mixed fractions

(D) Improper fractions

(35) Which of the following contains an improper fraction?

(A) 2/3, 5/7, 6/9 and 1/2

(B) 3/6, 1/4, 6/5 and 7/9

(C) 1/2, 6/8, 9/10 and 10/11

(D) 1/4, 2/7, 3/7 and 4/5

(36) Which of the following fractions can be converted to mixed fractions?

(A) Complex fractions

(B) Simple fractions

(C) Improper fractions

(D) Proper fractions

(37) Convert 14/11 to a mixed fraction.

(A) 1 1/3

(B) 1 2/3

(C) 1 3/11

(D) 2 3/11

(38) What is 6/5 as a mixed fraction?

(A) 1 2/5

(B) 1 1/2

(C) 1 4/5

(D) 1 1/5

(39) Find the sum of 4/5 and 1/5 in simplest terms.

(A) 5/5

(B) 7/5

(C) 1

(D) 6/5

(40) What is the sum of 2/3 and 4/5?

(A) 1 7/22

(B) 1 7/15

(C) 2 5/14

(D) 3 2/5

(41) Add 4/5 and 3/4.

(A) 1 11/20

(B) 3 4/5

(C) 1 3/20

(D) 2 13/20

(42) Find the difference between 3/4 and 5/6.

(A) 1/3

(B) 2/5

(C) 1/11

(D) 1/12

(43) Subtract 6/7 from 20/21.

(A) 2/21

(B) 3/21

(C) 7/22

(D) 5/22

(44) How do you identify the bigger fraction when performing a subtraction operation?

(A) By dividing both numbers by 2

(B) By converting the numbers to improper fractions

(C) By converting the numbers to decimal

(D) By estimating

(45) How do you divide a fraction?

(A) By dividing the fraction with the divisor

(B) By multiplying the fraction with the inverse of the divisor

(C) By dividing the fraction with any number between 1 and 9

(D) By subtracting the smaller fraction from the bigger fraction

(46) Divide 3/4 by 4.

(A) 3/16

(B) 4/16

(C) 11/16

(D) 13/16

(47) How do you multiply a fraction with another fraction?

(A) By multiplying the smaller fraction with the bigger fraction

(B) By multiplying the bigger fraction with the smaller fraction

(C) By multiplying the fractions together directly

(D) By multiplying the bigger fraction with the inverse of the smaller fraction

(48) Multiply 1/2 by 3/4.

(A) 3/5

(B) 4/7

(C) 3/8

(D) Undefined

(49) Differentiate between the division of fractions and the multiplication of fractions.

(A) Division of a fraction involves multiplying the fraction with the exact number, while the multiplication of a fraction involves multiplying the fraction with the inverse of the multiplier.

(B) To divide a fraction, multiply it by the inverse of the divisor, while the multiplication of a fraction is a direct operation.

(C) Division of a fraction involves dividing the fraction with its inverse, while the multiplication of a fraction involves multiplying the fraction with the inverse of the given multiplier.

(D) Division of a fraction involves multiplying the fraction with half of the inverse, while the multiplication of a fraction involves multiplying the fraction with the multiple of the given multiplier directly.

(50) How is fraction-to-decimal conversion done?

(A) By multiplying the fraction with its decimal equivalent

(B) By dividing the numerator with the denominator

(C) By multiplying the numerator with the denominator

(D) By dividing the numerator with the inverse of the denominator

(51) What is a ratio?

(A) The conversion of improper fractions to balanced fractions

(B) The comparison of two quantities or numbers

(C) The comparison of two unequal or uneven numbers

(D) The conversion of simple fractions to complex fractions

(52) Which of the following is not an operation that can be performed on ratios?

(A) Division

(B) Scaling

(C) Reduction

(D) None of the above

(53) What does ratio scaling involve?

(A) The conversion of a ratio to another by using a scaling value

(B) The multiplication of a ratio value by a scaling value

(C) The reduction of a ratio by a scaling value

(D) The elimination of the fractional part of a ratio number

(54) If there are 15 boys and 10 girls in a class, how many girls and boys are in four classes?

(A) 50 boys and 45 girls

(B) 70 boys and 60 girls

(C) 60 boys and 40 girls

(D) 80 boys and 65 girls

(55) Which of the following pairs of ratios are equal?

(A) 2/3 and 4/5

(B) 4/7 and 8/15

(C) 3/5 and 6/10

(D) 4/5 and 15/16

(56) What is the simple rule for testing ratio equivalency?

(A) Divide the two ratios by each other.

(B) Divide the two ratios by their inverses.

(C) Convert the two ratios to decimal numbers.

(D) Convert the two ratios to improper fractions.

Reading Test 1: Passages

Passage 1: The Role of Artificial Intelligence in Education

Over the years, artificial intelligence (AI) has touched practically every facet of human life. From medicine to the military, engineering and science, AI contributed in no small measure to the growth of these sectors. However, its uses are not restricted to those sectors. It is also a powerful tool in education. Let's take a look at the present and prospective uses of AI.

Grading is one of the most difficult tasks that teachers have to deal with. It is extremely time-consuming, especially for voluminous courses. AI can take the stress off teachers if it is incorporated into grading. It is efficient in grading multiple-choice questions and thus saves teachers the time they would have otherwise spent on such tedious work. It is expected that AI's uses will extend to grading essay questions in the future, enabling teachers to devote more time to teaching and less time to grading.

Individualized learning, another aspect of AI, is gradually gaining popularity. Through special software programs that are designed according to students' needs, a student can go over a topic as many times as needed to understand the subject, play educational games and use other resources to make learning a lot easier. This will have a huge impact on learning, comprehension and students' overall academic performance.

AI can also reduce the learning trial and error that some students experience. Sometimes, students' inability to figure out topics or lectures may frustrate them. This may discourage them from learning. Specialized computer programs and software can help them overcome the challenge. These programs will prove instrumental in helping kids learn at their own pace and figure things out before they attend lectures. It will enable them to put their fears behind them and take the bull by the horns, helping them become better students.

AI can also assist students in leveraging the power of instant feedback. This is crucial to academic success. Students can use apps and other resources to learn and get immediate feedback that highlights their weaknesses and strengths. Thus, they can work on their weaknesses while taking advantage of their strengths to improve their learning abilities.

Teachers who are using these teaching tools can also make learning less stressful and more impactful by creating flash cards and other study guides. These and other resources will increase a teacher's efficiency.

By removing boundaries, technology has opened the way for students from all over the world to study at their preferred educational institutes regardless of their location, even without being physically present in their schools. Thus students can choose a course of study that is not presently available in their country or region and study it online through AI. In view of this, everyone can dream of having the best education possible, without limitations.

AI is revolutionizing the education sector. In the future, the role of AI will be more defined as more students and teachers turn to it.

Passage 2: Why Is the Unemployment Rate Rising?

Unemployment is a global problem. From Asia to Africa, Europe to America, millions of working-age people struggle to make ends meet thanks to job scarcity across the globe. The impact of this problem on the world's economy cannot be overemphasized. What are the major causes of unemployment? Below are some common causes of job scarcity around the world.

Geographical immobility is one of the major causes of unemployment. Some unemployed people may not be able to relocate for a job. Someone looking for a job in New York may be unwilling or unable to relocate to Texas even if there are job opportunities there. Their reluctance may be due to health challenges, high cost of living and other related factors. This leads to geographical immobility, a prominent cause of unemployment for some people.

Changes in technology have contributed immensely to increasing unemployment rates. Thanks to AI, robots and other machines are being designed to replace humans based on the argument that robots are more efficient and less expensive. While this may be true, the consequence is that hundreds of thousands of people who are qualified for some roles cannot compete with these machines, so they lose out on prospective jobs. Hundreds of thousands of workers have lost their jobs to these highly efficient machines, increasing the number of unemployed people across the globe.

Job outsourcing is another contributing factor to unemployment. From time to time, companies move their production or manufacturing lines to other countries. When they do, their current staff are thrown into the workforce to compete with the already oversaturated market. The result is usually a jump in the number of unemployed people in the company's present location.

Low consumer demand may also drive unemployment rates. When a company experiences low consumer demand, it will record poor sales. If such a situation persists, the company may find itself running the business at a loss. Thus the company may lay off some workers. These people will scramble for the few job opportunities available and thereby cause unemployment rates to explode.

Every year, thousands of new graduates are thrown into the workforce. A significant number of these people may be unable to land a job for a wide range of reasons. While waiting for a job, they remain unemployed and contribute directly to the ever-increasing unemployment rates in the country. That is aside from people who take time off from work to raise a family or engage in other pursuits but later come back to join the workforce.

These and several other factors contribute in one way or another to the skyrocketing unemployment rates in the country, and by extension, the world.

Passage 3: The Impact of Virtual Reality on Tourism

Tourism is one of the fastest-growing industries in the world. Annually, millions of people take vacations to see landmark places across the globe, generating billions of dollars in revenue for the industry. Recently, virtual reality (VR) was introduced into tourism. What is the impact of this technology on the booming industry?

Travel agents are using this tool to make their job easier. According to Travel World VR, a New Jersey-based travel company, VR is an effective marketing tool that enables travel agents to promote tourism and market memorable travel experiences to potential tourists.

Through amazing cinematic VR and 360-degree videos, travel companies can promote attractive destinations around the world to their customers and thus inspire them to make travel plans.

Hotels are also leveraging VR to appeal to more clients by promoting their destinations. Customers can have a foretaste of what a hotel offers before booking accommodation. The interactive marketing experience has resulted in increased patronage for hotels, especially for travelers and tourists.

The restrictions placed on tourism by the current events in the world are a source of concern. With no specific date for the tourism industry to get back on its feet, fun-seekers can take advantage of VR to tour different parts of the world. From the comfort of your home, you can visit your favorite beaches and see tourist attractions in different geographical locations thanks to VR. The travel restrictions occasioned by the pandemic are not enough to deny you a golden opportunity to see the world virtually.

Since 2016, Skylights, a reputable airline, has set the pace in tourism marketing through VR. The airline offers its passengers in-lounge and in-flight VR experiences, a form of virtual entertainment that is designed to whet passengers' appetites by taking them through the world's famous tourist attractions.

The airline offers over 250 hours of movie content, ranging from documentaries to blockbusters, to give its customers memorable travel experiences. With its partnership with National Geographic, Warner Brothers, Lionsgate, Dream Works, 20th Century Fox and BBC, the airline is maximizing the opportunities offered by VR to expand its reach and create a memorable travel experience for its passengers.

Other airlines that have bought into this idea are Air France, British Airways and Garuda Indonesia. Time will tell how impactful VR will be on the travel industry, but from all indications, the industry will never remain the same as it takes advantage of VR to give tourists amazing content and experiences that will make them yearn for more.

Buttressing this, ResearchAndMarkets.com published a report that indicated VR offers the tourism industry the potential to give tourists extremely useful experiences that may support both natural and heritage preservation.

Reading Test 1: Questions

(1) Based on context in the passage, define *every facet.*

(A) Everywhere

(B) Everyone

(C) All aspects

(D) Everybody

(2) What does *in no small measure* mean?

(A) Significantly

(B) In small quantities

(C) Apparently

(D) Subtly

(3) Define *voluminous.*

(A) High volume

(B) Stressful

(C) Heavy workload

(D) None of the above

(4) Why is grading considered difficult?

(A) Because it takes time and energy

(B) Because the pay is not worth it

(C) Because it is boring

(D) Because it is underappreciated

(5) What is one limitation of AI grading at the moment?

(A) It cannot be used to grade multiple-choice questions.

(B) Its use is limited to grading essay questions.

(C) Only teachers with good computer skills can use it.

(D) It cannot grade essay questions.

(6) What is individualized learning?

(A) A type of learning designed by each individual

(B) A type of learning designed to meet the specific learning ability of each student

(C) A type of learning tailored to meet a group of students' learning objectives

(D) None of the above

(7) What features of AI make individualized learning possible?

(A) One-on-one teaching

(B) Group-based teaching

(C) Special software programs

(D) All of the above

(8) What does it mean to figure something out?

(A) Read it thoroughly

(B) Understand

(C) Overcome

(D) Procrastinate

(9) What is the danger of trial-and-error learning?

(A) It only works for elementary school students.

(B) Only people with special skills can use it.

(C) It discourages learning.

(D) It bores teachers.

(10) What is the meaning of *take the bull by the horns*?

(A) Reluctantly face a difficult situation

(B) Courageously face a difficult situation

(C) Patiently face a difficult situation

(D) Hurriedly face a difficult situation

(11) How does AI promote instant feedback?

(A) Students can receive immediate feedback when learning through some apps.

(B) Students can receive immediate feedback from their teachers who are using digital education tools.

(C) Students can receive immediate feedback from their school website.

(D) Parents can get involved and contact teachers with questions about grades.

(12) How has AI impacted global learning?

(A) It has made global learning more expensive.

(B) It has made global learning impossible.

(C) It has removed obstacles to global learning.

(D) It has helped strike a balance between local and global learning.

(13) Why is getting immediate feedback crucial to learning?

(A) It helps students make smarter choices.

(B) It helps students identify their strengths and weaknesses.

(C) It can determine a student's future.

(D) All of the above.

(14) How can teachers leverage the power of AI?

(A) By using it to create informative study guides

(B) By using it to monitor students' offline and online activities

(C) By using it to promote technology-dependent teaching

(D) By using it to encourage students to become tech-savvy

(15) How have international students benefited from the impact of AI on education?

(A) It opens the door to distance learning.

(B) It makes them better students.

(C) It helps them see the future of education.

(D) It comes in handy when preparing for examinations.

(16) What is one weakness of AI, as highlighted in the passage?

(A) It makes education readily available to people from all walks of life.

(B) It makes education expensive.

(C) It promotes technology-dependent education.

(D) None of the above.

(17) According to the passage, define *revolutionizing*.

(A) Creating a great change in the educational sector

(B) Creating a great change in school administration

(C) Creating a positive impact on learning

(D) Creating a significant change in teachers' employment policy

(18) How do teachers benefit from AI?

(A) It makes teaching less cumbersome for them.

(B) It makes teaching more fun and effective.

(C) It makes teaching more financially rewarding.

(D) It reduces the stress of going to a physical school for teaching.

(19) What can you deduce from the passage?

(A) Teaching is enjoyable only with the help of AI.

(B) Teachers who cannot handle AI will soon be out of a job.

(C) AI will have a massive positive impact on education, both now and in the future.

(D) AI will eliminate the need for physical schools.

(20) What is unemployment?

(A) Not having a satisfying job

(B) Not having a job befitting one's status

(C) Not having a job at all

(D) Working part time

(21) What does *unemployment is a global problem* mean?

(A) Unemployment is a problem among G-8 countries.

(B) Unemployment can be addressed by international organizations.

(C) Unemployment is a common problem among different countries.

(D) Unemployment will soon be eliminated.

(22) *Cannot be overemphasized* means what?

(A) It justifies the amount of emphasis.

(B) It does not justify the amount of emphasis.

(C) It should be discussed.

(D) It should not be discussed.

(23) Define *geographical immobility* as used in the passage.

(A) Loss of mobility

(B) Inability to move

(C) Absence of means of transportation

(D) Relocation problems

(24) What are some factors that can trigger geographical immobility?

(A) Poor road networks

(B) High cost of transportation

(C) High cost of living

(D) All of the above

(25) Is there a connection between unemployment and technological innovations?

(A) Yes, there is.

(B) No, there is no connection between them.

(C) It depends on an individual's perception.

(D) No one can determine the connection.

(26) How do some justify the replacement of human labor with machines?

(A) They consider machines to be more attractive.

(B) They consider machines to be more efficient.

(C) They consider humans to be more argumentative than machines.

(D) They consider humans to be too dependent on machines.

(27) How do machines contribute to the global unemployment rates?

(A) They create more corporate positions.

(B) They are more efficient than humans.

(C) They reduce the number of available jobs.

(D) B and C.

(28) What is job outsourcing?

(A) Relocating a part or all of a company's workforce to other countries

(B) Employing expatriates to take jobs currently handled by the locals

(C) Reducing the number of job opportunities available in a country

(D) Offering job opportunities to friends and family

(29) What is the connection between low consumer demand and unemployment?

(A) Low consumer demand leads to poor production.

(B) Low consumer demand leads to low sales.

(C) Low consumer demand has zero impact on unemployment.

(D) Low consumer demand reduces unemployment rates.

(30) Which of the following is the opposite of *scramble for*?

(A) Compete for

(B) Line up for

(C) Search for

(D) Available to all

(31) Define *workforce* according to the passage.

(A) Unemployable people

(B) Unemployed people

(C) Working people

(D) Unskilled workers

(32) Which of the following people can increase unemployment rates in a country?

(A) Someone who retires from a job to set up her own business

(B) Someone who joins the entertainment industry to showcase his skills

(C) Someone who just returned to the workforce after being away for years

(D) All of the above

(33) Define *oversaturated* as used in the passage.

(A) Having many people searching for fewer jobs

(B) Having more-qualified people competing with less-qualified people for the same job

(C) Having more graduates looking for jobs

(D) None of the above

(34) What is the opposite of *prominent*?

(A) Important

(B) Noticeable

(C) Conspicuous

(D) Less known

(35) What does the idiom *to make ends meet* mean?

(A) To move from one location to another

(B) To afford the luxuries of life

(C) To afford the basic necessities of life

(D) To barely get by

(36) What is the meaning of *the consequences* according to the passage?

(A) The result of unemployment

(B) The result of replacing humans with machines

(C) The result of geographical immobility

(D) The result of scarce employment opportunities

(37) What can you deduce from the passage?

(A) Several factors are responsible for increasing unemployment rates.

(B) Many unemployed people are not ready to work.

(C) There are enough jobs for those who are passionate about working.

(D) Only a handful of people know the best way to get their dream jobs.

(38) What is the opposite of *skyrocket*?

(A) Appreciate

(B) Increase

(C) Reduce

(D) Elevate

(39) Why is tourism considered a fast-growing industry?

(A) It generates huge revenue and attracts millions of tourists.

(B) It is controlled by influencers and powerful people.

(C) It is supported by automakers.

(D) It employs more employees than other industries.

(40) How do travel agents take advantage of virtual reality?

(A) They use it to promote tourism and memorable travel experiences.

(B) They use it to employ more workers.

(C) They use it to establish a good working relationship with stakeholders in the tourism industry.

(D) All of the above.

(41) How do travel companies use VR to promote their businesses?

(A) Through 360-degree and cinematic VR videos

(B) Through video games and cartoons

(C) By creating VR-dependent destinations for tourists

(D) By bringing VR experts into the industry

(42) According to the passage, what does *foretaste* mean?

(A) A taste of VR

(B) An idea of what hotels have to offer

(C) The landmark achievements of the hotels

(D) Previous hotel users' experiences

(43) How do hotels attract more customers through VR?

(A) They create special packages for VR users.

(B) They take potential customers on a virtual trip around the hotels.

(C) They give discounts to customers who subscribe to their VR packages.

(D) They allow their customers to use their VR free of charge.

(44) How does VR benefit potential tourists in view of the world's current pandemic situation?

(A) They can make plans for the reopening of the tourism industry via VR.

(B) They can use VR to create short and attractive videos.

(C) They can visit tourist attractions virtually.

(D) They can recollect their past tourist experiences via VR.

(45) What does *has set the pace* mean?

(A) Following predefined rules and regulations

(B) Making appreciable progress

(C) Being the first to use VR

(D) Being the best at using VR for tourism promotion

(46) What does it mean to *whet someone's appetite*?

(A) To make them lose their appetite

(B) To make them crave more

(C) To indulge them

(D) None of the above

(47) What is the opposite of *virtual*?

(A) Technology-inspired

(B) Technology-dependent

(C) Real

(D) Fake

(48) What are other terms for *booming*?

(A) Growing and successful

(B) Losing customers and sales

(C) Performing poorly

(D) Not breaking even

(49) What is implied by *from the comfort of your home*?

(A) Bravely

(B) Sleepily

(C) Effortlessly

(D) Conveniently

(50) How can airlines attract more customers via VR?

(A) By creating documentaries and movies to attract their customers

(B) By slashing flight fees

(C) By encouraging more VR users

(D) By partnering with VR companies

(51) What word in the passage is the opposite of *less appreciable*?

(A) Significant

(B) Amazing

(C) Expand

(D) Heritage

(52) What expression in the passage can you substitute for *seize an opportunity*?

(A) Have a significant impact

(B) Take advantage of

(C) Buy into the idea

(D) None of the above

(53) What word or phrase can accurately substitute for *buttressing* as used in the passage?

(A) Working in favor of

(B) Supporting

(C) Countering

(D) Cooperating with

(54) What does *bought into this idea* mean as used in the passage?

(A) Believed in

(B) Ignored

(C) Making financial contributions to

(D) Testing

(55) *To expand its reach* means what?

(A) Increase number of employees

(B) Add more routes

(C) Reach more potential customers

(D) Increase income

(56) Define *memorable.*

(A) Cannot be easily forgotten

(B) Can be easily forgotten

(C) None of the above

(D) A and B

Writing Test 1: Questions

(1) Define sentence structure.

(A) The confusing organization of sentences

(B) The grammatical arrangement of sentences

(C) The logical organization of sentences

(D) The psychological organization of sentences

(2) Which of the following are not types of sentences?

(A) Simple sentences and complex sentences

(B) Complex sentences and compound-complex sentences

(C) Compound sentences and complex sentences

(D) Primary sentences and secondary sentences

(3) Define a simple sentence.

(A) A type of sentence that is made up of a single clause, single subject and it can have two predicates

(B) A type of sentence that is made up of a single clause and it can have two subjects or two predicates

(C) A type of sentence that is made up of a single clause, single predicate and single subject

(D) A type of sentence that is made up of two independent clauses and one dependent clause

(4) What constitutes a complex sentence?

(A) An independent clause and one or two dependent clauses

(B) Two independent clauses and one or two dependent clauses

(C) One or two independent clauses and one or two dependent clauses

(D) One or two independent clauses and multiple dependent clauses

(5) What is the independent clause in this sentence: "She left for the beach after doing the dishes"?

(A) She left for the beach

(B) After doing the dishes

(C) None of the above

(D) A and B

(6) Under what condition is it mandatory to use an indefinite article?

(A) For specific nouns

(B) For specific pronouns

(C) For general nouns

(D) For general pronouns

(7) What type of sentence is this: "Because I couldn't eat my food cold, I heated it up in the microwave"?

(A) Simple sentence

(B) Complex sentence

(C) Compound sentence

(D) Compound-complex sentence

(8) What is the most popular sentence structure?

(A) Subject, subject, verb

(B) Subject, verb, object

(C) Subject, object, verb

(D) Subject, adverb, preposition

(9) "Although I live some distance away from school, I enjoy walking." How many independent clauses are in this sentence?

(A) Two

(B) One

(C) Zero

(D) None of the above

(10) Which of the following sentences shows the order of arrangement in writing where the subject comes first?

(A) The boy was bitten by the snake.

(B) The little girl was beaten by the bully.

(C) The driver drove the long bus recklessly.

(D) The bicycle was handled recklessly.

(11) Why should you use short sentences?

(A) Short sentences are easy to write.

(B) So that your readers will criticize your material.

(C) Short sentences help readers to stay focused on the material.

(D) So that you don't appear to be showing off to your readers.

(12) How can you master the art of linking words?

(A) By using coordinating conjunctions randomly

(B) By connecting points together logically

(C) By using phrasal verbs and idiomatic expressions

(D) By using special word connectors

(13) Which of these pairs of words or phrases is ideal for indicating similarity?

(A) In contrast and nevertheless

(B) Likewise and furthermore

(C) To exemplify and moreover

(D) On the other hand and in addition

(14) Define a sentence fragment.

(A) An incomplete sentence

(B) An incomplete adjective

(C) A parts-of-speech usage error

(D) A grammatical and logical error

(15) Which of the following is a sentence fragment?

(A) She is going home after the lecture.

(B) Bolu and Tope are a set of twins.

(C) When the principal arrives.

(D) The boy is as tall as his father.

(16) How do comma splices occur?

(A) When a sentence contains too many commas

(B) When a sentence contains an insufficient number of commas

(C) When two independent clauses are joined with a comma that is not grammatically correct

(D) When a sentence contains too many commas and other grammatical elements

(17) Which of the following is a dependent clause?

(A) Although he is handsome.

(B) She is not the only girl in the class.

(C) Dancing is fun.

(D) None of the above.

(18) How can you correct comma splices?

(A) By using many commas in a sentence

(B) By reducing the number of commas in a sentence

(C) By using the appropriate punctuation mark

(D) By using autocorrecting software programs and applications to fix the issue

(19) Under what condition is splitting a sentence into two ideal for fixing comma splices?

(A) For a subordinate clause and two independent clauses

(B) For two independent clauses

(C) For two dependent clauses

(D) For a dependent clause and at least two independent clauses

(20) "Lions are not herbivores, they are carnivores." Identify the error in the sentence.

(A) Dangling modifier

(B) Missing adverbial conjunction

(C) Comma splice

(D) Run-on

(21) Rewrite this sentence: “She wanted to go out and because she was sick, she needed help.”

(A) She wanted to go out and because she was sick, she needed help.

(B) She wanted to go out and because she was sick she needed help.

(C) She wanted to go out. Because she was sick, she needed help.

(D) She wanted to go out but because she was sick, she needed help.

(22) Where should a conjunction be placed to correct a comma splice in a sentence?

(A) Immediately after the comma

(B) Immediately before the comma

(C) Two words before the comma

(D) Two words after the comma

(23) “I may miss the date, the weather isn’t encouraging.” How do you fix the comma splice error in this sentence?

(A) By replacing the comma with a conjunction

(B) By using a semicolon

(C) By introducing a conjunction

(D) All of the above

(24) What are run-ons?

(A) Sentence structure errors that arise from the merging of two or more dependent clauses without proper punctuation

(B) Sentence structure errors that arise from the merging of two or more independent clauses without proper punctuation

(C) Sentence structure errors that arise from the merging of two or more independent clauses without the appropriate figures of speech

(D) Sentence structure errors that arise from the merging of two or more dependent clauses without the appropriate figures of speech

(25) How do you handle two independent clauses in a sentence to correct run-ons?

(A) Split the sentence into three different sentences

(B) Introduce special figures of speech

(C) Split the sentence into two different sentences

(D) Introduce phrasal verbs and conjunctions

(26) Correct the run-on error in this sentence: "She is preparing for her forthcoming examination will travel when she is done."

(A) She is preparing for her forthcoming examination than will travel when she is done.

(B) She is preparing for her forthcoming examination then will travel when she is done.

(C) She is preparing for her forthcoming examination, but will travel when she is done.

(D) She is preparing for her forthcoming examination. She will travel when she is done.

(27) How do you fix a run-on if the clauses express connected ideas?

(A) Introduce a semicolon

(B) Introduce a conjunction

(C) Introduce a phrasal verb or an idiomatic expression

(D) Separate the sentence with a coordinating conjunction

(28) What should you focus on while editing your work?

(A) Your choice of words and syntax

(B) The sentence structure and syntax

(C) None of the above

(D) A and B

(29) What editing practice is most effective?

(A) Start and complete the editing process as fast as you can

(B) Break the editing process into sections

(C) Edit the material twice

(D) Go through the material repeatedly before you start editing

(30) Which of the following is a complete collection of proper nouns?

(A) Toyota, Margaret, France, *New York Post*

(B) Alex, dog, Canada and computer

(C) Pen, Felix, book and goat

(D) None of the above

(31) Nouns that are not physical and cannot be seen are known as what?

(A) Collective nouns

(B) Invisible nouns

(C) Abstract nouns

(D) Concrete nouns

(32) What are the two types of concrete nouns?

(A) Collective and selective

(B) Countable and uncountable

(C) Simple and complex

(D) Compound and complex

(33) Identify the odd pair of nouns from the list below.

(A) Flock, team and board

(B) Crowd, forest and pair

(C) Fleet, crowd and choir

(D) Board, bouquet and animal

(34) Which of the following is not a complete set of abstract nouns?

(A) Emotions, concepts and traits

(B) Feelings, emotions and concepts

(C) Feelings, emotions and traits

(D) Emotions, traits and objects

(35) Identify the odd set from the lists below.

(A) and, but, because

(B) Crowd, army, school

(C) *New York Post*, Toyota, BMW

(D) None of the above

(36) Which of the following collective nouns is used for a group of fish?

(A) School

(B) Group

(C) Team

(D) Collection

(37) What is a group of ants called?

(A) Collection

(B) Army

(C) Herd

(D) Pack

(38) Which of the following sentences contains an adjective?

(A) He was so happy to see his mother.

(B) The couple has a home.

(C) The girls are playing with their toys.

(D) None of the above.

(39) Identify the sentence that contains a concrete noun.

(A) Annie is watching TV.

(B) She is angry.

(C) The program will be aired tomorrow.

(D) Happiness is free.

(40) "Due to the enormity of his crime, the hit-and-run driver fled." What type of sentence is this?

(A) A simple sentence

(B) A complex sentence

(C) A compound-complex sentence

(D) A compound sentence

Essay 1: Should Smoking in Public Be Banned?

According to the Centers for Disease Control and Prevention (CDC), 34.2 million US adults, or 13.7 percent, were active cigarette smokers in 2018. Almost three-quarters of these adults, 74.6 percent, can't even contemplate not smoking each day. Evidently, smoking is a social problem that requires urgent attention across the country.

Sadly, these addicted smokers do not limit their habit to indoors. They satisfy their urge everywhere—parks, bus stops, cinemas, stadiums and other public places—without giving a second thought to others. In view of this, the government should consider banning smoking in public in the United States for several reasons.

Smoking in public turns nonsmokers into secondhand smokers. While this may seem harmless, the reverse is the case. The Cleveland Clinic has performed studies that show 20 to 30 minutes of exposure to cigarette smoke may trigger excess blood clotting and equally increase a victim's risk of stroke and heart attack.

Exposure to secondhand smoke for two hours increases the nonsmoker's risk of arrhythmia or irregular heartbeat and increases the individual's susceptibility to a heart attack and/or fatal cardiac arrest. Prolonged exposure to cigarette smoke may also increase the risk of developing some serious health conditions, such as lung disease, lung cancer, heart disease and other smoking-related disorders.

Aside from humans, animals are also at risk of developing serious health conditions as a result of their exposure to cigarette smoke. Thus, when you are taking your dog for a walk, and you smoke, you stand the risk of exposing your pet to health risks associated with secondhand smoking.

In public places where smoking is allowed, such as restaurants, bars and other establishments, others have to deal with the lingering odor of cigarette smoke hours after the smoker has left. Other users of these public places may also have to contend with cigarette smoke on their clothes, even for days after visiting such places.

Litter reduction is another important reason why the government should consider banning smoking in public. Annually, cigarette stubs account for a significant portion of litter in public places in the United States. Banning public smoking will reduce this problem considerably.

The economic impact of exposure to secondhand smoke is another reason why the government should consider banning public smoking. The National Library of Medicine published a report that estimated the total cost of treating ailments resulting from secondhand smoking in Minnesota in 2008 to be $228.7 million. That was roughly $45 per Minnesota resident. You can imagine the total cost for the entire United States in that year.

Granted, there may be counterarguments in favor of public smoking. Some people are of the opinion that banning smoking in public places takes away people's freedom. They consider a national health stance against public smoking as tantamount to infringing on an individual's freedom of choice. However, in view of the overwhelming evidence that public smoking is not only dangerous to the smoker but also endangers nonsmokers, and in particular infants and children, there is enough evidence to consider banning smoking in public.

Essay 1 Questions

(1) Which of the following statements is true?

(A) Smoking is harmless.

(B) Smoking affects smokers only.

(C) Smoking affects nonsmokers.

(D) Smoking is fun.

(2) What is the argument against banning smoking in public?

(A) It is harmless.

(B) It takes away people's freedom.

(C) It generates revenue for the government.

(D) All of the above.

Essay 2: Online Dating: Is it for You?

The quest for true love has taken many people to the internet. They seek solace in online dating with the hope of meeting Prince or Princess Charming. While some have memorable, successful experiences to share, some have nothing but horror stories. If you are contemplating online dating, is it actually for you?

Before you take the next step, consider some basic facts about online dating.

Online Dating Is Time-Consuming

When you first start using Tinder or any other online dating app, you will have fun shopping for the right person to shoot you with Cupid's arrow. Over time, it will dawn on you, though, that you are spending too much time on the app, especially if you are not comfortable with the people you have met so far.

Even when you find the man or woman of your dreams, you will spend hours communicating with him or her online, devoting your time to keeping the relationship going. Online dating will take a substantial part of your time.

Dashed Expectations

Dashed expectations is another issue you must contend with if you experiment with internet-based relationships. Do not be surprised if your date does not look like what you expect when you meet. This is a common experience among online daters and is one of the reasons why some people are averse to online dating.

Weirdos

You have to deal with weirdos, too. Some people hide behind the privacy offered by online dating sites to disguise how strange they are. Women may be amazed at the number of unsolicited genitals that await them in their inbox. That is aside from other shocking experiences they may have when dating online.

But online dating is not all negative. Here are some online dating pros you should also consider when making your decision.

No Dearth of Suitors

When engaging in online dating, you will not ever run out of suitors. Many people may be interested in your profile. Hopefully, you will find someone who checks all the boxes to sweep you off your feet.

It Is Convenient

When dating offline, you sometimes have to sacrifice convenience to keep the relationship going. Conversely, online dating offers you an opportunity to date at your convenience. You can engage in meaningful conversation with your lover without giving a second thought to the threatening rainfall or the weather. You can even date online while in the kitchen or the bathroom. Thus, online dating takes the physical stress of offline dating off your shoulders.

It Is Cost-Effective

Have you ever tried a matchmaker? They do not come cheap, and some may charge as much as $5,000 to connect you with a potential lover. However, aside from data and your time, you will not spend much on online dating. This makes it a more convenient and cheaper option, especially if you are on a budget.

Online dating obviously has its pros and cons. Before you give it a shot, consider if you can deal with the cons while taking full advantage of the pros.

Essay 2 Questions

(1) How does the passage suggest that online dating is time-consuming?

(A) It takes time to keep a relationship going.

(B) It takes time to find a suitable partner.

(C) None of the above.

(D) A and B.

(2) What does *check all the boxes* mean?

(A) Meet your criteria

(B) Be ready to spend the rest of their life with you

(C) Be willing to take care of you

(D) All of the above

Mathematics Test 1: Answers & Explanations

(1) (B) Countable numbers.

Whole numbers are countable numbers, such as 1, 2, 3, 4 and so on. Numbers such as 123, 6,790 and 10,235 are examples of whole numbers.

(2) (C) They are positive numbers only.

Whole numbers are positive numbers only. Thus, while 12, 5,644 and 873 are examples of whole numbers, -34, -129 and -321 are not.

(3) (B) Positive and negative numbers.

Integers include both positive and negative numbers. Hence, numbers such as -23, 56, 71, -456 are included.

(4) (C) -2/9, 76, 23 and 18.

-2/9 is not an integer because it is a fraction. Integers must be whole numbers or their opposites.

(5) (B) 510.

Reorganize the numbers and ensure proper alignment. Start the addition from the right and pay attention to carries as you work progressively toward the left.

(6) (C) 196.

Reorganize the numbers and ensure proper alignment. Start the addition from the right and pay attention to carries as you work progressively toward the left.

(7) (D) Reorganize the numbers to ensure their alignment.

You should pay attention to how you organize numbers when performing addition, especially if the addends are not of the same value. This is the first step.

(8) (B) From the right-hand side.

This is very important for accurate calculation. If students start the addition from the left hand, they will get the wrong answer.

(9) (C) The order of arrangement.

When you are adding integers, it is important to organize the integers so that you are adding like places.

(10) (B) 132.

Determine the bigger and smaller of the two figures first. Then, subtract the smaller integer from the bigger integer, starting from the right-hand side.

(11) (D) When the number to be subtracted is smaller than the number it is being subtracted from.

You can only subtract a smaller number from a bigger one. However, if you must subtract a bigger number from a smaller number, you borrow from the next number to the left.

(12) (A) Addition and subtraction of integers start from the right, while division starts from the left.

To perform addition or subtraction, start from the right and work toward the left. The reverse is the case when dividing integers.

(13) (D) 101.

Start from the right. Find the number of times that 5 can divide 5. Then, move to 0. How many times can 5 divide 0? Lastly, divide the last 5 by 5.

(14) (D) Combine the next number in the numerator with it.

If the divisor cannot divide the numerator, combine the next number in the numerator with the first number to produce a two-digit number.

(15) (C) 675.

Reorganize the numbers and start adding from the right, using the last number of the multiplier, 5. Then use 1 to continue the multiplication, also starting from the right.

(16) (A) From the right.

Multiplication of integers should start from the right, like addition and subtraction.

(17) (C) Numbers with a whole and a fractional part.

Decimals are numbers with a whole part and a fractional part. Some examples of decimals are 23.45, 0.89, 56.78 and so on.

(18) (B) Whole number.

The number before the decimal point is the whole number part, while the number after the decimal is the fractional part.

(19) (C) None of the above.

All operations that can be performed on integers can be performed on decimal numbers too. Hence, you can add, subtract, multiply and divide decimals.

(20) (B) 49.13.

The addition is similar to addition of integers. However, while reorganizing the numbers, take note of the decimal positions and add the numbers accordingly.

(21) (B) Alignment of numbers.

You should pay attention to the alignment of the numbers when performing any operation on decimal numbers.

(22) (C) To ensure proper alignment of the numbers.

Zero is sometimes added to decimal numbers to ensure proper alignment. For instance, if a number with two decimal values is added to another one with three decimal values, the 0 will give proper alignment.

(23) (C) 623.77.

Identify the bigger number. Reorganize the numbers and start the subtraction from the right-hand side. When reorganizing the numbers, consider the decimal values.

(24) (C) 89.22.

Identify the bigger number. Reorganize the numbers and start the subtraction from the right-hand side. When reorganizing the numbers, consider the decimal values.

(25) (D) 19.56.

Start the division from the left and work toward the right until you are done. Consider the number of decimal places when writing your answer.

(26) (D) 20.50.

Start the division from the left and work toward the right until you are done. Consider the number of decimal places when writing your answer.

(27) (C) 1,327.20.

Start the multiplication from the right. When you are done, add the values and consider the decimal value when writing your final answer.

(28) (A) 153.78.

Start your multiplication from the right using 4. When you are done, use 3. Since there are a total of three decimal values in the two numbers, count three numbers from the right and place your decimal point there.

(29) (B) 9.88.

First, add 56.12 and 78.34 while paying attention to decimal values. Then, subtract 12.34 from the answer.

(30) (B) 7/10.

Since there is a single number after the decimal point, turn the decimal value into an integer and divide it by 10. The number of zeros after 1 is determined by the decimal value of the given number.

(31) (A) 4/5.

Since there is a single number after the decimal point, turn the decimal value into an integer and divide it by 10. Then, express your answer in lowest form.

(32) (C) 3/5.

Since there is a single number after the decimal point, turn the decimal value into an integer and divide it by 10. Then, express your answer in lowest terms.

(33) (D) None of the above.

There are mixed numbers, improper fractions, proper fractions, simple fractions and complex fractions. Therefore, the answer is none of the above.

(34) (D) Improper fractions.

In an improper fraction, the numerator is bigger than the denominator.

(35) (B) 3/6, 1/4, 6/5 and 7/9.

Only option B contains an improper fraction: 6/5.

(36) (C) Improper fractions.

Improper fractions are converted into mixed fractions by dividing the numerator by the numerator. The answer is usually a whole number and a remainder. The remainder/denominator forms the fractional part of the mixed fraction.

(37) (C) 1 3/11.

Divide 14 by 11. You get 1 because there is just one 11 in 14. The remainder is 3. 3/11 is the fractional part.

(38) (D) 1 1/5.

Divide 6 by 5. You get 1 because there is just one 5 in 6. The remainder is 1. 1/5 is the fractional part.

(39) (C) 1.

When adding two fractions with similar denominators, simply add the numerators while the denominator remains the same. Simplify your answer if possible.

(40) (B) 1 7/15.

Since they are different denominators, find a common denominator: 15. How many 3s in 15? Five. Multiply 2 by 5. How many 5s in 15? Three. Multiply 4 by 3. Then 10 + 12/15. Add the terms and simplify if possible.

(41) (A) 1 11/20.

Since they are different denominators, find a common denominator: 20. How many 5s in 15? Four. Multiply 4 by 4. How many 4s in 20? Five. Multiply 5 by 3. Then 16 + 15/20. Simplify if possible.

(42) (D) 1/12.

Determine the bigger and smaller numbers by converting both into decimals. The decimal number closer to 1 represents the bigger number. Then, subtract the smaller from the bigger number.

(43) (A) 2/21.

Determine the bigger and smaller numbers by converting both into decimals. The decimal number closer to 1 represents the bigger number. Then, subtract the smaller from the bigger number.

(44) (C) By converting the numbers to decimals.

Determine the bigger and smaller numbers by converting both into decimals. The decimal number closer to 1 represents the bigger number.

(45) (B) By multiplying the fraction with the inverse of the divisor.

To divide a fraction, multiply it with the inverse of its divisor. For instance, to divide 1/4 by 2/3, multiply 1/4 by 3/2.

(46) (A) 3/16.

To divide 3/4 by 4, multiply it by the inverse of 4, which is 1/4. Then you have (3 * 1)/(4 * 4) = 3/16.

(47) (C) By multiplying the fractions together directly.

To multiply two fractions, multiply them directly. It is a straightforward operation without using any inverse.

(48) (C) 3/8.

To multiply 1/2 by 3/4, you have (1 * 3)/(2 * 4) = 3/8.

(49) (B) To divide a fraction, multiply it by the inverse of the divisor, while the multiplication of a fraction is a direct operation.

The difference between dividing and multiplying a fraction is that to divide a fraction, you multiply it by the inverse of the divisor; the multiplication of a fraction is a direct operation.

(50) (B) By dividing the numerator with the denominator.

To convert a fraction to a decimal, divide the numerator with the denominator until nothing more is left to divide.

(51) (B) The comparison of two quantities or numbers.

Ratios deal with the comparison of two numbers or quantities. They define how many times a specific number is contained in another given number.

(52) (D) None of the above.

Several operations, such as division, scaling and reduction, can be performed on ratios.

(53) (B) The multiplication of a ratio value by a scaling value.

Scaling a ratio is a mathematical operation that involves multiplying the ratio values by a specific number known as the scaling value.

(54) (C) 60 boys and 40 girls.

Boys: girls for 1 class = 15:10

For four classes, multiply the ratio by 4.

Therefore, 4 classes = (15:10)4.

Thus, 4 classes = 60:40.

There are 60 boys and 40 girls in four classes.

(55) (C) 3/5 and 6/10.

3/5 and 6/10 is the only pair, or equal ratio, in the set. If you multiply 3/5 by 2, the answer is 6/10. If you divide 6/10 by 2, the result is 3/5. So, they are equal ratios.

(56) (C) Convert the two ratios to decimal numbers.

To test the equivalency of two ratios, convert them to decimals. If they share the same decimal values, they are equal. For instance, 3/5 = 0.6 and 6/10 = 0.6.

Reading Test 1: Answers & Explanations

(1) (C) All aspects.

According to the passage, *every facet* means *all aspects*. Thus, *every facet of human life* means *every aspect of human life*.

(2) (A) Significantly.

In no small measure means *significantly*. According to the passage, AI has made an immense contribution to all aspects of human life.

(3) (C) Heavy workload.

Voluminous, according to the context, means *a lot*, so you can infer *heavy workload* as the meaning. Hence, teaching contains a heavy workload that includes teaching and grading.

(4) (A) Because it takes time and energy.

Grading takes time and energy. Depending on the number of students, it may take a teacher hours or days to complete grading.

(5) (D) It cannot grade essay questions.

AI can be used to grade multiple-choice questions but cannot be used to grade essay questions. However, experts are working toward using AI to grade essay questions in the future.

(6) (B) A type of learning designed to meet the specific learning ability of each student.

Students have different learning abilities. When considering this, a teacher will focus on individualized learning that factors in students' diverse learning abilities and styles.

(7) (C) Special software programs.

Through special software programs designed according to students' needs, a student can go over a topic as many times as needed to understand it. Students can also play educational games and use other resources to make learning a lot easier. This is how AI allows for individualized learning.

(8) (B) Understand.

To figure something out means *to understand it.*

(9) (C) It discourages learning.

When students are learning by trial and error, they may lose interest if they repeatedly struggle with a topic.

(10) (B) Courageously face a difficult situation.

Take the bull by the horns is an idiom. It means *to courageously face a difficult situation.*

(11) (A) Students can receive immediate feedback when learning through some apps.

Students can use AI to get immediate feedback that highlights their weaknesses and strengths. Thus, they can work on their weaknesses while taking advantage of their strengths to improve their learning abilities.

(12) (C) It has removed obstacles to global learning.

By removing boundaries, AI has opened the way for students from all over the world to study at their preferred educational institutes, regardless of their location, even without being physically present in their schools.

(13) (B) It helps students identify their strengths and weaknesses.

Getting immediate feedback is beneficial to students. It helps them identify their weaknesses and strengths. Thus, they can work on improving on their weaknesses while capitalizing on their strengths.

(14) (A) By using it to create informative study guides.

Teachers can use AI to create informative study guides, such as graphs and infographics.

(15) (A) It opens the door to distance learning.

Students can choose a course of study that is not presently available in their country or region and study it online through AI. In view of this, everyone can dream of having the best education possible, without limitations.

(16) (D) None of the above.

The passage does not mention any cons of using AI. Rather, it highlights its major benefits, such as promoting effective teaching, making distance learning possible, etc.

(17) (A) Creating a great change in the educational sector.

Revolutionizing, as used in the passage, means *creating a great change in the education sector*. Thus, AI may change the future of education as its impact on the sector becomes more pronounced.

(18) (B) It makes teaching more fun and effective.

As teachers use modern teaching tools, thanks to AI, teaching becomes less tedious and more fun.

(19) (C) AI will have a massive positive impact on education, both now and in the future.

You can deduce from the passage that, in view of the numerous uses of AI in the education sector, it is believed that the technology will have a massive and pronounced impact on education, both now and in the future.

(20) (C) Not having a job at all.

Unemployment means not having a job. Working part time, not having a satisfying job, or not having a job befitting one's status does not qualify as unemployment.

(21) (C) Unemployment is a common problem among different countries.

The word *global* means *affecting the whole world*. Thus, *unemployment is a global problem* means it affects every country in the world.

(22) (A) It justifies the amount of emphasis.

When you overemphasize something, you're placing too much emphasis on it. Hence, *cannot be overemphasized* means that something justifies the amount of emphasis placed on it.

(23) (D) Relocation problems.

Geographical immobility does not refer to the loss of mobility or absence of means of transportation. Rather, as used in the passage, it refers to relocation problems.

(24) (C) High cost of living.

Some factors that may trigger geographical immobility include high cost of living and health challenges. These factors may prevent some unemployed people from relocating in search of job opportunities.

(25) (A) Yes, there is.

Changes in technology have contributed immensely to increasing unemployment rates. Robots and other machines are designed to replace human workers.

(26) (B) They consider machines to be more efficient.

Machines are designed to replace human workers because the proponents of such an idea believe that machines are more efficient and less expensive than humans.

(27) (D) B and C.

Machines contribute to global unemployment rates by reducing the number of available jobs and being more efficient than humans. Thus, they are preferred over people in some industries.

(28) (A) Relocating a part or all of a company's workforce to other countries.

From time to time, companies outsource jobs, meaning they move their production or manufacturing lines to other countries. When they do, their current employees are thrown into the workforce.

(29) (B) Low consumer demand leads to low sales.

Low consumer demand may push unemployment rates. When a company experiences low consumer demand, it will record poor sales and may decide to lay off some workers.

(30) (D) Available to all.

To scramble for something means to struggle or compete for it. On the other hand, when something is available to all, it means there's an ample supply and people do not have to struggle to get it.

(31) (B) Unemployed people.

Workforce refers to all the people in an area who are available for work. Thus they are not working people or unskilled workers.

(32) (C) Someone who just returned to the workforce after being away for years.

Some people leave their jobs to set up a business, raise a family or pursue higher education. If such a person returns to the workforce, unemployment rates may increase.

(33) (A) Having many people searching for fewer jobs.

When the number of job seekers exceeds the number of available jobs, the job market is oversaturated.

(34) (D) Less known.

Prominent means something is noticeable or well-known. Thus its opposite is *less known* or *not conspicuous*.

(35) (C) To afford the basic necessities of life.

When you make ends meet, you are earning enough to afford your basic needs, but you cannot enjoy any luxuries.

(36) (B) The result of replacing humans with machines.

A consequence is the result of an event. Thus, according to the passage, the consequences are the replacing of humans with machines.

(37) (A) Several factors are responsible for increasing unemployment rates.

It can be deduced from the passage that several factors, such as geographical immobility and increasing numbers of graduates, are responsible for increasing unemployment rates.

(38) (C) Reduce.

When something skyrockets, it increases at an alarming rate. In the passage, *skyrocket* refers to the rate at which unemployment keeps increasing. Hence, its opposite is *reduce.*

(39) (A) It generates huge revenue and attracts millions of tourists.

Tourism is considered a fast-growing industry because it attracts millions of tourists from around the globe and thus generates billions of dollars in revenue.

(40) (A) They use it to promote tourism and memorable travel experiences.

VR is an effective marketing tool that enables travel agents to promote tourism and market memorable travel experiences to potential tourists.

(41) (A) Through 360-degree and cinematic VR videos.

Through amazing cinematic VR and 360-degree videos, travel companies can promote attractive destinations across the globe and thus inspire their customers to make travel plans.

(42) (B) An idea of what hotels have to offer.

A foretaste gives a small idea of what a situation will be like on a larger scale. According to the context of the word's use in the passage, it means an idea of what hotels have to offer.

(43) (B) They take potential customers on a virtual trip around the hotels.

With VR, hotels around the world are attracting more customers by taking them on a virtual tour of their properties.

(44) (C) They can visit tourist attractions virtually.

From the comfort of their homes, tourists can visit their favorite beaches, see tourist attractions in different geographical locations and have fun while doing it, thanks to VR.

(45) (C) Being the first to use VR.

Someone who sets the pace has set a standard for others to emulate. As used in the passage, it means the companies are the first to use VR for promotional purposes, leaving others to emulate them.

(46) (B) To make them crave more.

When you whet someone's appetite, you make them crave more of what you give them. Thus, by using VR, airlines want passengers to crave more of the experience.

(47) (C) Real.

Virtual means *an imitation of the thing described*. Thus, it is not real, but is created to seem real. Therefore, the opposite of *virtual* is *real*.

(48) (A) Growing and successful.

When a business or an economy is said to be *booming*, it means it is growing and successful, or thriving.

(49) (D) Conveniently.

When something is from the comfort of your home, it means it is convenient. You do not have to stress yourself by actually going to the beaches or tourist attractions, as stated in the passage.

(50) (A) By creating documentaries and movies to attract their customers.

Airlines can attract more customers via VR by creating documentaries and movies.

(51) (A) Significant.

Something that is significant is important enough to be noticed or have an effect. On the other hand, something less appreciable is not considered important.

(52) (B) Take advantage of.

Take advantage of can replace *seize an opportunity* as used in the passage because they are synonyms.

(53) (B) Supporting.

To buttress an argument means to provide supporting evidence. Hence, *supporting* can replace *buttressing*, according to the passage.

(54) (A) Believed in.

When you buy into something, you believe in the idea. In this case, the airlines did not only believe in VR as a promotional tool; they also supported the idea.

(55) (C) Reach more potential customers.

When a company expands its reach, it reaches out to more potential clients. Per the reading passage, companies are using the power of VR to achieve this.

(56) (A) Cannot be easily forgotten.

Something that is memorable cannot be easily forgotten. *Memorable* and *unforgettable* are synonyms.

Writing Test 1: Answers & Explanations

(1) (B) The grammatical arrangement of sentences.

Sentence structure is the grammatical arrangement of a sentence. This focuses on the arrangement of the subjects, verbs and other elements of your writing.

(2) (D) Primary sentences and secondary sentences.

Primary sentences and secondary sentences are not types of sentences. The types of sentences are simple, compound, complex and compound-complex.

(3) (C) A type of sentence that is made up of a single clause, single predicate and single subject.

A simple sentence has only one clause, subject and predicate.

(4) (A) An independent clause and one or two dependent clauses.

A complex sentence consists of an independent clause and one or two dependent clauses.

(5) (A) She left for the beach.

"She left for the beach" is the independent clause because it is meaningful if it stands alone. The same cannot be said for "after doing the dishes."

(6) (C) For general nouns.

When referring to specific nouns, the definite article is used. The indefinite article is used for general nouns.

(7) (B) Complex sentence.

This is a complex sentence because the first part of the sentence is a dependent clause, while the other part is an independent clause.

(8) (B) Subject, verb, object.

The most popular sentence structure is subject, verb, object.

(9) (B) One.

The sentence contains one independent clause: "I enjoy walking."

(10) (C) The driver drove the long bus recklessly.

While the other options start with the object, option C starts with the subject, followed by the verb and the object.

(11) (C) Short sentences help readers to stay focused on the material.

Short sentences will help your audience focus better on the material. Beware of overdependence on short sentences, though. This can cause your writing to sound choppy.

(12) (B) By connecting points together logically.

You can master the art of linking words if you cultivate the habit of connecting points together logically at every opportunity until it becomes second nature.

(13) (B) Likewise and furthermore.

You can connect points in your passages with words such as *similarly, in addition, also, furthermore, moreover* and *likewise* when indicating similarity.

(14) (A) An incomplete sentence.

Incomplete sentences are referred to as fragments. They consist of a subject without a predicate.

(15) (C) When the principal arrives.

While all the other options are complete sentences, option C is incomplete and is an example of a sentence fragment.

(16) (C) When two independent clauses are joined with a comma, that is not grammatically correct.

When two independent clauses are joined with a comma, that is not grammatically correct and is known as a comma splice.

(17) (A) Although he is handsome.

"Although he is handsome" is an incomplete sentence. It depends on other clauses to convey a meaning. Thus it is a dependent clause.

(18) (C) By using the appropriate punctuation mark.

An effective strategy for correcting a comma splice is to use the appropriate punctuation mark.

(19) (B) For two independent clauses.

One of the solutions for fixing comma splices is splitting the sentence into two. If the sentence contains two independent clauses, a semicolon or a period may be used.

(20) (C) Comma splice.

The sentence contains two independent clauses that are separated by a comma. Furthermore, the sentence does not have a conjunction. It contains a comma splice.

(21) (C) She wanted to go out. Because she was sick, she needed help.

This is a good way to fix a comma splice. Simply break the sentence into two meaningful parts.

(22) (A) Immediately after the comma.

You can introduce a coordinating conjunction into the sentence to correct the error. The conjunction should be placed immediately after the comma.

(23) (B) By using a semicolon.

To correct the comma splice, you should separate the two clauses with a semicolon. Alternatively, you can break the sentence into two separate sentences.

(24) (B) Sentence structure errors that arise from the merging of two or more independent clauses without proper punctuation.

Another common sentence structure error is the run-on, when two or more independent clauses are joined without proper punctuation.

(25) (C) Split the sentence into two different sentences.

Run-ons can be corrected with the same techniques that correct sentence fragments. If there are two independent clauses in the sentence, separate them into two different sentences.

(26) (D) She is preparing for her forthcoming examination. She will travel when she is done.

The run-on sentence has been split into two independent sentences to fix the error.

(27) (A) Introduce a semicolon.

If the two clauses in the run-on express connected ideas, use a semicolon to join them and fix the error.

(28) (D) A and B.

When editing a piece of writing, check your choice of words, syntax and structure.

(29) (B) Break the editing process into sections.

When you are finished writing something, break the editing process into sections. This enables you to be thorough with the editing.

(30) (A) Toyota, Margaret, France, *New York Post.*

This is a complete set of proper nouns.

(31) (C) Abstract nouns.

Abstract nouns are not visible to the physical eye, but they can be felt and experienced. Emotions, traits and concepts are examples of abstract nouns.

(32) (B) Countable and uncountable.

Concrete nouns can be both countable or uncountable.

(33) (D) Board, bouquet and animal.

While other answer options consist of all collective nouns, option D does not, as *animal* is not a collective noun.

(34) (D) Emotions, traits and objects.

Emotions, traits and objects are not abstract nouns. While emotions and traits are abstract, objects can be seen and touched.

(35) (D) None of the above.

There is no odd set in the list of answers. Option A is a set of conjunctions, option B is a set of collective nouns and option C is a set of proper nouns.

(36) (A) School.

A group of fish (a collective noun) is called a school.

(37) (B) Army.

A group of ants is called an army of ants. Thus, *army* is the collective noun for ants.

(38) (A) He was so happy to see his mother.

This sentence contains the adjective *happy*.

(39) (A) Annie is watching TV.

Abstract nouns are visible. In this sentence, *TV* is an object that can be seen. Thus, the sentence contains a concrete noun.

(40) (B) A complex sentence.

It is a complex sentence because it contains an independent clause and a dependent clause.

Essay 1 Answers & Explanations

(1) (C) Smoking affects nonsmokers.

Smoking in public turns nonsmokers inadvertently into secondhand smokers. This statement is true. Smoking may have a profound, negative impact on bystanders' health, according to health experts.

(2) (B) It takes away people's freedom.

Some believe that banning smoking in public places takes away people's freedom. They consider a national stance against public smoking as tantamount to infringing on an individual's freedom of choice.

Essay 2 Answers & Explanations

(1) (D) A and B.

According to the passage, online dating is time-consuming because it takes time to find the right partner. Keeping a relationship going requires a reasonable amount of time, too.

(2) (A) Meet your criteria.

All online dating platform users have some specific criteria they want in a prospective partner. When someone checks all the boxes, it means they meet your criteria.

Mathematics Test 2: Questions

(1) Identify the pair of equal ratios.

(A) 2/3 and 4/5

(B) 3/5 and 7/8

(C) 5/6 and 10/12

(D) 8/10 and 15/20

(2) If the ratio of male and female passengers in a vehicle is 5/7, find the equivalent ratio.

(A) 10/12

(B) 15/21

(C) 15/30

(D) 21/25

(3) Reduce 16/20 to the lowest terms.

(A) 8/10

(B) 5/6

(C) 4/5

(D) 2/3

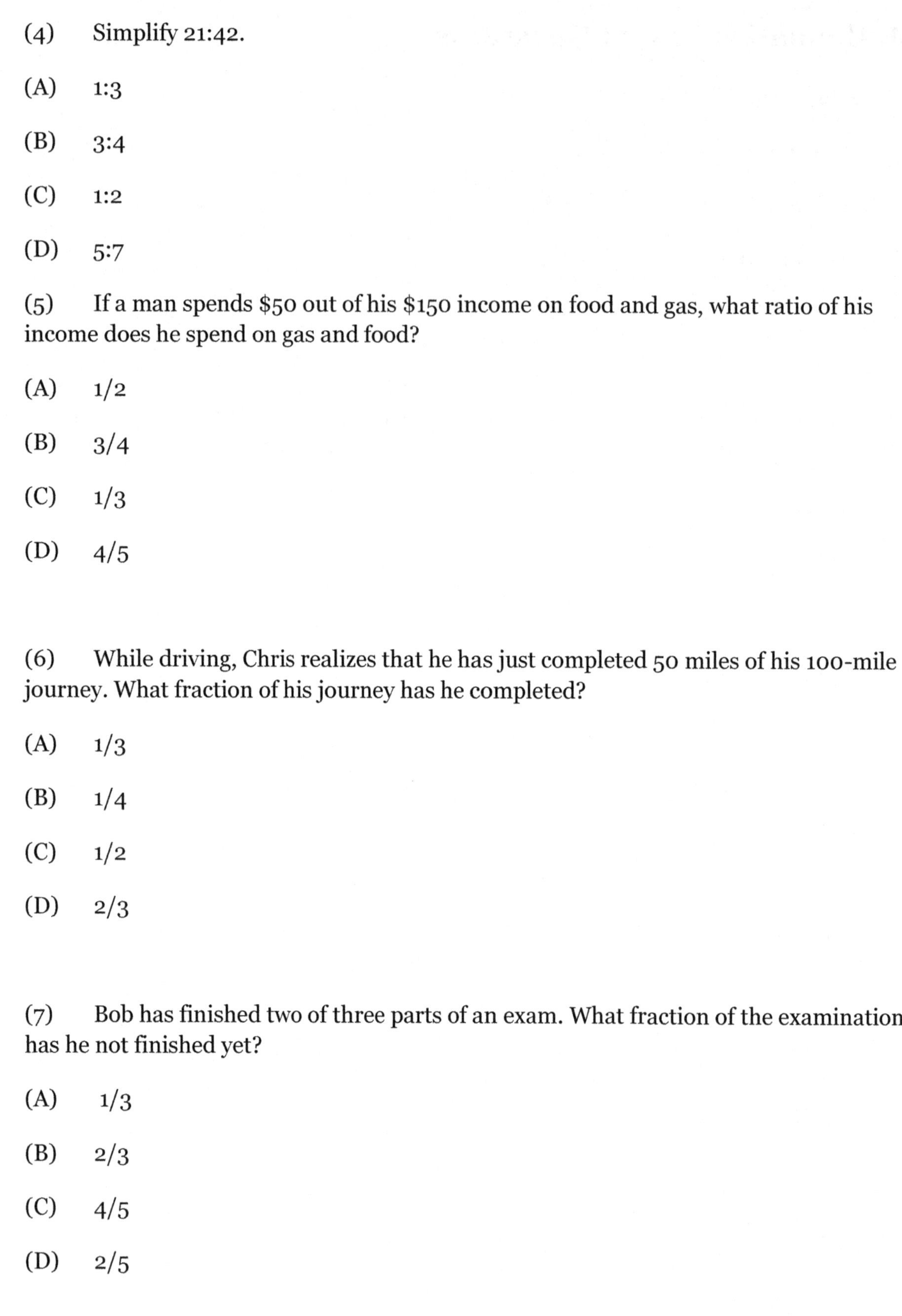

(4) Simplify 21:42.

(A) 1:3

(B) 3:4

(C) 1:2

(D) 5:7

(5) If a man spends $50 out of his $150 income on food and gas, what ratio of his income does he spend on gas and food?

(A) 1/2

(B) 3/4

(C) 1/3

(D) 4/5

(6) While driving, Chris realizes that he has just completed 50 miles of his 100-mile journey. What fraction of his journey has he completed?

(A) 1/3

(B) 1/4

(C) 1/2

(D) 2/3

(7) Bob has finished two of three parts of an exam. What fraction of the examination has he not finished yet?

(A) 1/3

(B) 2/3

(C) 4/5

(D) 2/5

(8) How do you determine the proportionality of two values?

(A) By dividing them by each other

(B) By dividing them by their difference

(C) By cross-multiplying the two values

(D) By subtracting them from each other

(9) Determine the proportionality of 2/3 and 14/21.

(A) They are proportional.

(B) They are not proportional.

(C) Their proportionality cannot be determined.

(D) Their proportionality depends on several factors.

(10) Find the value of x if 2/3 is proportional to x/21.

(A) 8

(B) 14

(C) 10

(D) 15

(11) Find the value of y if y/3 is proportional to 24/36.

(A) 3

(B) 5

(C) 2

(D) 7

(12) What does 60% mean?

(A) The proportionality of 60 and 100

(B) The reversibility of 60

(C) 60 expressed with respect to 100

(D) None of the above

(13) In a bus of 60 passengers, 20 are female and the rest are male. Express the male passengers as a percentage of the total passengers.

(A) 66.7%

(B) 60%

(C) 68.75%

(D) 59.50%

(14) Express 15/20 as a percentage.

(A) 60%

(B) 70%

(C) 80%

(D) 75%

(15) What percentage of 20 is 12?

(A) 80%

(B) 70%

(C) 75%

(D) 60%

(16) Which of the following is true?

(A) 1 meter = 120 centimeters

(B) 1 meter = 80 centimeters

(C) 1 meter = 100 centimeters

(D) 1 meter = 150 centimeters

(17) Convert 1,500 kilometers to miles.

(A) 932 miles

(B) 942 miles

(C) 920 miles

(D) 900 miles

(18) Convert 520 pounds to kilograms.

(A) 239 kilograms

(B) 236 kilograms

(C) 240 kilograms

(D) 230 kilograms

(19) A table tennis court is 50 feet long. Approximately how long is the tennis court in centimeters?

(A) 1,519 centimeters

(B) 1,524 centimeters

(C) 1,419 centimeters

(D) 1,319 centimeters

(20) The foundation of a house is 100 square feet. Convert the measurement to square meters.

(A) 9.3 square meters

(B) 9.7 square meters

(C) 9.6 square meters

(D) 9.0 square meters

(21) A man covered 1,200 miles on his motorcycle. What approximate distance did he cover in kilometers?

(A) 1,931 kilometers

(B) 1,850 kilometers

(C) 1,893 kilometers

(D) 1,873 kilometers

(22) If a vehicle weighs 8,000 kilograms, what is its approximate weight in pounds?

(A) 3,930 pounds

(B) 18,950 pounds

(C) 14,000 pounds

(D) 17,637 pounds

(23) Round 1,567 to the nearest 10.

(A) 1,500

(B) 1,570

(C) 1,580

(D) 1,600

(24) What is 12,345 to the nearest hundred?

(A) 12,500

(B) 12,400

(C) 12,800

(D) 12,300

(25) What is the value of 5,627 when rounded to the nearest 100?

(A) 5,600

(B) 5,700

(C) 5,500

(D) 6,600

(26) Round 56.23 to the nearest tenth.

(A) 56.3

(B) 56.33

(C) 56.2

(D) 56.20

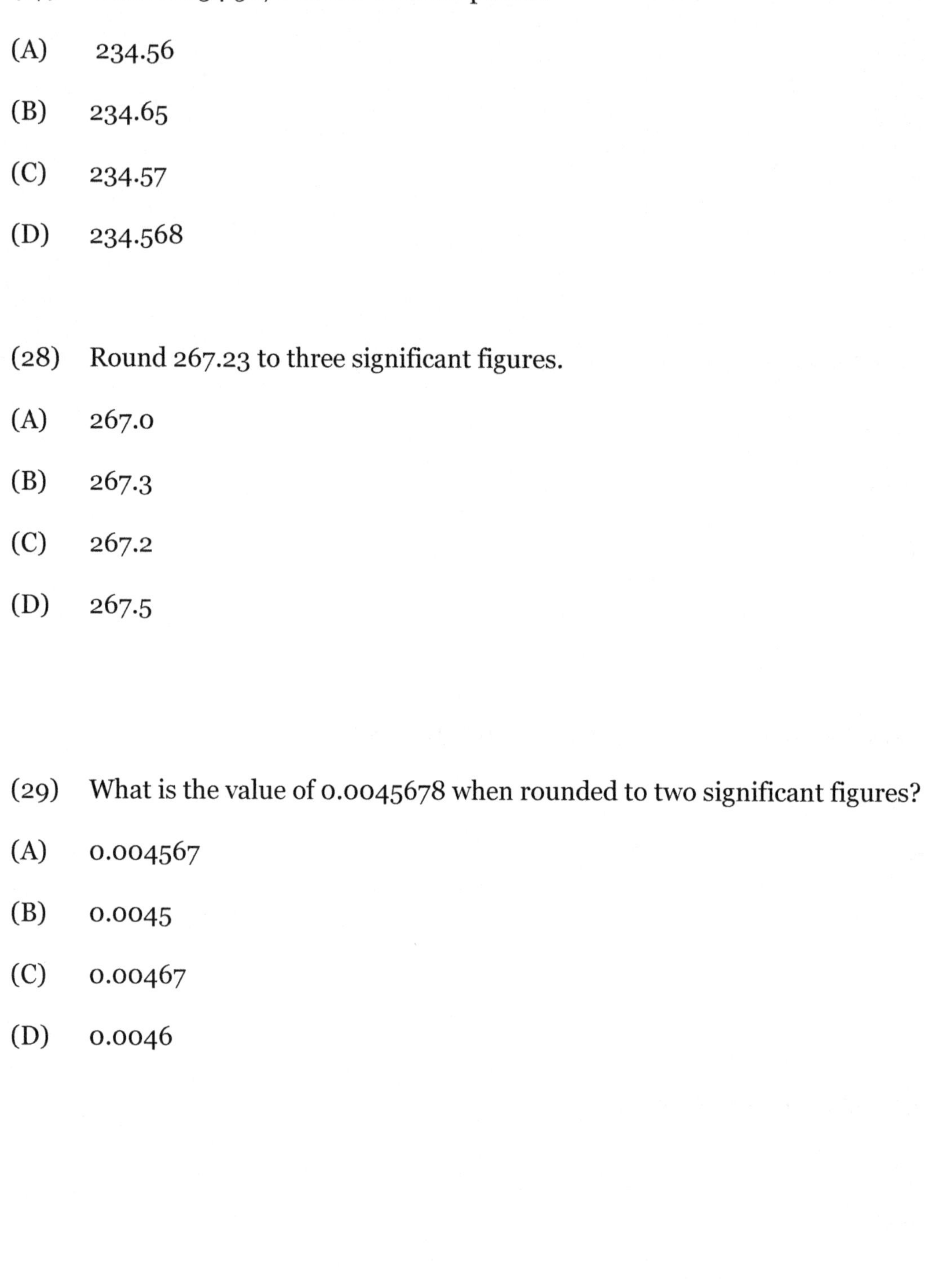

(27) What is 234.5678 to two decimal places?

(A) 234.56

(B) 234.65

(C) 234.57

(D) 234.568

(28) Round 267.23 to three significant figures.

(A) 267.0

(B) 267.3

(C) 267.2

(D) 267.5

(29) What is the value of 0.0045678 when rounded to two significant figures?

(A) 0.004567

(B) 0.0045

(C) 0.00467

(D) 0.0046

(30) Which of the following are not common algebraic terms?

(A) Like terms and coefficients

(B) Unlike terms and coefficients

(C) Corresponding values and coefficients

(D) None of the above

(31) What are like terms?

(A) Algebraic expressions with the same variables and exponents

(B) Algebraic expressions with the same coefficients

(C) Algebraic expressions with corresponding values

(D) Algebraic expressions with the same variables and corresponding values

(32) What is the sum of 2ab + 4xy + xy +3ab?

(A) 3ab + 3xy

(B) 3ab + 5xy

(C) 5ab + 5xy

(D) 5ab + 3xy

(33) Add 5bc + 8 cd + 3ay +3bc + 2ay + 2xy.

(A) 8bc + 8cd + 5ay + 2xy

(B) 6bc + 8cd + 5ay + 2xy

(C) 8bc + 7cd + 5ay + 2xy

(D) 8bc + 8cd + 8ay + 2xy

(34) Simplify the expression 8ab + 3bc + 10xy – 2ab – 4xy.

(A) 6ab + 3bc + 6xy

(B) 6ab + 5bc + 6xy

(C) 6ab + 3bc + 5xy

(D) 6ab + 6bc + 6xy

(35) Subtract 5ab + 4cd from 10ab + 8cd.

(A) 5ab + 3cd

(B) 10ab + 5cd

(C) 5ab + 5cd

(D) 5ab + 4cd

(36) Divide 45ab by 5b.

(A) 9ab

(B) 9b

(C) 9a

(D) 10ab

(37) Divide $36b^2$ by 12b.

(A) $3b^2$

(B) $24b^2$

(C) 24b

(D) 3b

(38) Multiply (a + 2) by (a + 3).

(A) $a^2 + 7a + 6$

(B) $a^2 + 6a + 5$

(C) $a^2 + 5a + 6$

(D) $a^2 + 5a + 5$

(39) Multiply (a + 4) by (a + 3).

(A) $a^2 + 7a - 12$

(B) $a^2 + 7a + 12$

(C) $a^2 + a - 12$

(D) $a^2 - 7a + 12$

(40) What are two-dimensional shapes?

(A) Shapes that have two measurable dimensions—the area and the circumference

(B) Shapes that have two measurable dimensions—the volume and the circumference

(C) Shapes that have two measurable dimensions—the length and the height

(D) Shapes that have two measurable dimensions—the length and the width

(41) Which of the following pairs is not a complete set of two-dimensional shapes?

(A) Sphere, cuboid and circle

(B) Circle, square and pentagon

(C) Rectangle, pentagon and circle

(D) Quadrilateral, triangle and pentagon

(42) Define a square.

(A) A geometrical shape with four right angles and two equal sides.

(B) A geometrical shape with four right angles and four equal sides.

(C) A geometrical shape with four obtuse angles and two equal sides.

(D) A geometrical shape with four acute angles and two equal sides.

(43) Which of the following is not correct about a rhombus?

(A) It is a parallelogram.

(B) It has two to four lines of symmetry.

(C) The opposite sides are parallel.

(D) The opposite angles are right angles.

(44) What are three examples of quadrilaterals?

(A) Rectangles, rhombuses and trapezoids

(B) Circles, rhombuses and trapezoids

(C) Cylinders, squares and kites

(D) Parallelograms, circles and kites

(45) Which of the following are not examples of a triangle?

(A) Isosceles and scalene

(B) Acute and obtuse

(C) Equilateral and isosceles

(D) Acute and octane

(46) Define obtuse triangle.

(A) A triangle with all angles equal to 90 degrees

(B) A triangle with one angle equal to 90 degrees

(C) A triangle with one angle greater than 90 degrees

(D) A triangle with the sum of the angles equal to 360 degrees

(47) What is the sum of the angles of a triangle?

(A) 90 degrees

(B) 180 degrees

(C) 270 degrees

(D) 360 degrees

(48) Differentiate between isosceles triangles and right-angle triangles.

(A) An isosceles triangle has two equal sides and angles, while one of the angles of a right-angle triangle is 90 degrees.

(B) A right-angle triangle has two equal sides and angles, while one of the angles of an isosceles triangle is 90 degrees.

(C) An isosceles triangle has three equal sides and angles, while one of the angles of a right-angle triangle is 90 degrees.

(D) An isosceles triangle has four equal sides and angles, while one of the angles of a right-angle triangle is 60 degrees.

(49) What is the Pythagorean Theorem?

(A) The square of the adjacent side of a right triangle is equal to the sum of the squares of the other sides of the triangle.

(B) The square of the hypotenuse side of a right triangle is equal to the sum of the squares of the other sides of the triangle.

(C) The square of the opposite side of a right triangle is equal to the sum of the squares of the other sides of the triangle.

(D) The square of the shortest side of a right triangle is equal to the sum of the squares of the other sides of the triangle.

(50) What is the longest side of a right-angle triangle called?

(A) The base

(B) The opposite

(C) The hypotenuse

(D) The perpendicular

(51) Find the size of the hypotenuse of a right triangle with a 3 cm base and a 4 cm perpendicular.

(A) 6 cm

(B) 5 cm

(C) 8 cm

(D) 2 cm

(52) If the length of the hypotenuse of a right triangle is 10 cm and the base is 8 cm, calculate the length of the opposite side.

(A) 6 cm

(B) 7 cm

(C) 12.8 cm

(D) 12 cm

(53) Find the size of the perpendicular side of a right triangle with an 8 cm hypotenuse and a 5 cm base.

(A) 8 cm

(B) 7.25 cm

(C) 6.25 cm

(D) 9.4 cm

(54) What formula guides Pythagorean triples?

(A) $c^2 = a^2 + b^2$

(B) $c^2 = a^2 - b^2$

(C) $c^2 = a^2 / b^2$

(D) $c^2 = a^2 * b^2$

(55) Which of the following are Pythagorean triples?

(A) 3, 4 and 5

(B) 6, 8 and 12

(C) 5, 7 and 10

(D) 2, 4 and 7

(56) What are five-sided and six-sided polygons called, respectively?

(A) Parallelograms and pentagons

(B) Parallelograms and hexagons

(C) Polygons and pentagons

(D) Pentagons and hexagons

Reading Test 2: Passages

Passage 1: The Importance of an Online Presence for Your Business

In this digital age, many entrepreneurs are creating an online presence for their businesses. They are creating websites, social media pages and other materials to take their businesses to every part of the world. If you are a business owner, there are several reasons why you should consider giving your business an online presence. Let's consider some of these reasons.

By creating websites and social media accounts for your business, you are giving it needed exposure. The days of limiting your business to your local environment are gone. Today, rather than concentrate on selling your products or services to people in your immediate environment, you have the entire world as your marketing environment.

Having an online presence makes it easier for customers to reach you at their convenience. People in different parts of the world may come across your products or services when searching for related services or products. With a couple of clicks on your website, potential and existing customers can see what you have to offer. They may order your services or products from their locations without actually contacting you personally, even when you are asleep. That is the power of an online presence.

Building relationships with potential and existing customers is easier through an online presence. You can interact and share meaningful information with them via your social media accounts and gradually build a lasting business relationship. For instance, if you have an impressive social media presence and are always available to answer questions from your customers, offer them valuable tips and get to know them better, you can take your business to the next level. As you add a human dimension to your business, people will trust you more, and such a relationship will also have a positive impact on your business.

In a competitive market, there is no better way to stand out and capture the attention of potential customers than by making your brand readily available to them through your social media platforms and website. Otherwise, if customers cannot easily get in touch with your business, they will look for better alternatives. Easy access to your business will boost sales. Conversely, if your business is not easily accessible, sales will be negatively affected.

The stiff competition in the business world demands that you do everything possible to have an edge over your competitors. Otherwise, your business may not survive.

Passage 2: Top Freelancing Skills in 2020 and Beyond

For years, many professionals have taken to freelancing to showcase their skills and make ends meet. Working from the convenience of their homes or offices, they offer their services to several clients without actually being on the payroll of a specific client or company. Nor are these freelancers chained to nine-to-five jobs.

If you are considering joining the millions of freelancers across the globe, here are the top freelancing skills that are in high demand.

Writing

With millions of websites hosted on the internet, freelance writers are having a field day putting their skills to work to ensure that people always have the latest information available at the click of a button. These professionals are working behind the scenes to give people up-to-date news and information via blogs, websites, podcasts, magazines and more. Thus, if you have the necessary writing skills, you may consider freelance writing and help fill the need for competent writers for consumers who look to the internet and other resources for the latest information for personal, professional or academic uses.

Logo Design

A logo is an integral part of business branding. Business owners create identities for their businesses with their trademarked logos. Hence there is a huge demand for logo designers. From websites to other forms of branding, you can put your skills to good use by becoming a logo designer.

Web Design

Web design is one of the most sought-after services in the world, thanks to the millions of websites that populate the internet. Entrepreneurs and organizations want to give their businesses an online presence, so they create websites for their brands to enable them to reach out to potential customers and clients, their locations notwithstanding.

If you are a skilled web designer, you can tap into this need and create a regular source of income. If you do not have web design skills, you can learn the art within a couple of months and quickly begin earning money.

Social Media Marketing

Business owners are fully aware of the potential impact of social media on their businesses. That is why they hire professional social media marketers to promote their brands. If you are a competent social media marketer, you can consider freelancing as a side hustle or your main hustle, depending on your circumstances.

The more time and dedication you invest in learning these skills, the better freelancer you will become—and that may translate into regular jobs.

Passage 3: Top Social Media Tricks to Help You Grow Your Business

The importance of social media as a marketing tool cannot be overemphasized. Since the introduction of social media marketing, businesses have leveraged its far-reaching effects to take their business to every nook and cranny of the earth.

However, while some people have success with their social media promotions, others have nothing to show for their efforts. If you are concerned about getting the best result from your social media promotion efforts, here are some practical tips you can use to grow your business.

Use Dynamic Videos to Boost Facebook Conversion

Videos have proven over the years to be the undisputed leader in Facebook advertising. With billions of monthly active users, Facebook is a powerful marketing platform. You can reach your target audience and create more impact by including short promotional videos to boost your Facebook Ads conversion. With Facebook's Dynamic Ads, you can use videos to deliver personalized advertising to prospective consumers.

Create Personalized Content

For promotional purposes, you must create personalized content to share with your audience on social media platforms. Since each platform differs from the others, study each platform and understand what will boost the effectiveness of your promotion. Then create content that your audience can identify with.

For instance, using trending tags on Twitter with the content you specifically design for that platform will increase its chances of reaching more readers, although such tags are ineffective on Facebook. This highlights the importance of understanding what will boost your promotion on each platform and creating content that is tailored for each social media platform.

Update Your Social Media Accounts Regularly

When running a personal social media account, you can afford to go for weeks without updating it. However, you must update your business social media accounts regularly to ensure that your audience is familiar with the new products or services you are offering. Even if you do not have new products or services, interacting with your customers regularly is a great way to build and sustain your business relationship with them. Otherwise, you may lose your customers to competitors that use social media more adeptly.

Learn from Your Competitors

You are not the only service provider in your line of business. And your product is not the only one on the market. A great way to get ahead of your competitors is to study them. What are they doing differently that is giving them good results? Once you understand this, use that as a template to develop a better product or service for your audience.

Social media is a powerful tool that can have a positive impact on your business. With these practical tips, you can leverage its potential to take your business to the next level.

Reading Test 2: Questions

(1) Define *digital age.*

(A) A period of time when technology is extensively used

(B) A period of time that is dependent on digital watches and cameras

(C) A period of time characterized by zeros and ones

(D) All of the above

(2) Who are entrepreneurs?

(A) Investors

(B) Digital marketers

(C) Website designers

(D) Business people

(3) Define the expression *What have you.*

(A) Everything being equal

(B) In a similar manner

(C) And so on

(D) In lieu of

(4) Which of the following is not an avenue to give your business an online presence?

(A) Website

(B) Twitter

(C) Facebook

(D) Skype

(5) What is one business problem that good social media promotion can help you overcome?

(A) Limited customer base

(B) Rent renewal

(C) Threat of competitors

(D) All of the above

(6) When is the "off time" when you are promoting your business online?

(A) Between 10:00 p.m. and 12:00 a.m.

(B) Between 12:00 a.m. and 5:00 a.m.

(C) Throughout the night

(D) No off time

(7) What is the biggest benefit of promoting your business online?

(A) You have fewer employees.

(B) You have a global market to explore.

(C) You will not be bothered by your customers.

(D) You will spend less money on physical offices.

(8) How can you build business relationships digitally?

(A) By communicating regularly with your customers

(B) By tweeting business-related information when you have new products or services

(C) By creating business accounts for promotional purposes

(D) By paying influencers to help you run your business accounts

(9) What is branding?

(A) Promoting your business to make it attractive to potential and existing customers

(B) Raising enough capital to list your business on the local exchange market

(C) Selling some shares of your company to interested investors

(D) Soliciting assistance from angel investors

(10) Why is branding important to business?

(A) It enables people to identify your business.

(B) It helps you raise capital for your business.

(C) It helps you leverage the power of the internet.

(D) All of the above.

(11) Define *competitive* as used in the passage.

(A) With fewer competitors

(B) With strong competition

(C) Prone to attacks from competitors

(D) Free of competition

(12) What does *stand out* as used in the passage mean?

(A) Staying outside a building

(B) Being better than your competitors

(C) Selling or offering a new product or service

(D) Having enough financial power to beat the competition

(13) *Have an edge over* means what?

(A) Sharpening a knife

(B) Being bigger

(C) Being in a better position

(D) Having more employees

(14) What is the danger of being too far away from your customers?

(A) They cannot communicate with you easily.

(B) They will look for more convenient alternatives.

(C) None of the above.

(D) A and B.

(15) How can you use social media to sustain your customers' interest?

(A) By sharing valuable tips with them

(B) By getting to know them better

(C) None of the above

(D) A and B

(16) What does it mean to *add a human dimension* to your business?

(A) You hire more humans than machines to run your business.

(B) You deal with your customers as humans, not just as a source of income.

(C) You hire human resource personnel to handle your business.

(D) You direct your promotion toward humans.

(17) *The days of limiting your business to your local environment are gone* means what?

(A) The practice is outdated.

(B) Such a practice never existed.

(C) Businesses that used such marketing approaches went out of business.

(D) Such a practice may come back in the future.

(18) Which other word can replace *conversely*?

(A) Additionally

(B) Invariably

(C) In other words

(D) Taking everything into consideration

(19) What does *freelancing* mean?

(A) Working from home

(B) Not working for a particular employer

(C) Working at your convenience

(D) Working part time

(20) Why are freelance writers needed?

(A) Because of the incompetence of the print media

(B) Because there is a deficiency of qualified writers

(C) Because of the proliferation of websites

(D) All of the above

(21) *Having a field day* as used in the passage means what?

(A) Exploring certain theories

(B) Enjoying abundant opportunities

(C) Operating in a lucrative field

(D) Having an emotional moment

(22) *Working behind the scenes* is what type of expression?

(A) Synecdoche

(B) Onomatopoeia

(C) Idiomatic

(D) Personification

(23) In which of the following industries are freelancers not needed?

(A) Blogs and websites

(B) Podcasts and YouTube

(C) Magazines and websites

(D) None of the above

(24) Why do businesses use customized logos?

(A) To show off their wealth

(B) To show they are the best

(C) For branding

(D) To beautify their websites

(25) What two factors determine the success or failure of a logo designer?

(A) Age and interest

(B) Availability and skill levels

(C) Years of experience and tools used

(D) Versatility and age

(26) Logos are used in all except which of the following?

(A) Souvenirs and websites

(B) GIFs and videos

(C) Social media assets and animation

(D) None of the above

(27) Why is there a growing need for website designers?

(A) They are cheaper to hire.

(B) They are readily available.

(C) There is an increasing number of websites.

(D) Websites experience low numbers of traffic.

(28) Businesses are creating websites for what purpose?

(A) To meet registration requirements

(B) For promotional purposes

(C) To remain in business

(D) To beat competition

(29) What are trademarked logos?

(A) Special logos

(B) 3D logos

(C) Personalized logos

(D) Abstract logos

(30) Which of the following is an advantage of freelancing?

(A) It allows you to work at your own pace and convenience.

(B) It allows you to overcome your limitations.

(C) It portrays you as a professional.

(D) It is less demanding.

(31) Why do businesses need social media marketers?

(A) To create social media accounts for them

(B) To give them presentations on why social media can be negative

(C) To help them promote their businesses on social media platforms

(D) To teach them how to do daily tasks without social media

(32) When will freelancing no longer exist?

(A) When all websites and blogs have been populated with content

(B) In 2030

(C) When the internet no longer exists

(D) Never

(33) What should you consider if you wish to become a freelancer?

(A) Time

(B) Years of experience

(C) Skills

(D) Number of available job opportunities

(34) What does *side hustle* mean?

(A) A hobby

(B) Another source of income aside from your regular job

(C) Something you do on weekends only

(D) Something you do only during the holidays

(35) Freelancing is limited to what category of people?

(A) Senior citizens

(B) Stay-at-home mothers

(C) Middle-aged men

(D) People with the required skills

(36) Which of the following is a nine-to-five job?

(A) Driving

(B) Teaching

(C) Corporate job

(D) Contract job

(37) What can you deduce from the passage about freelancing?

(A) Anyone with the required skills can become a freelancer.

(B) Freelancing offers an opportunity to beat unemployment.

(C) None of the above

(D) A and B

(38) What type of expression is *every nook and cranny*?

(A) Hyperbole

(B) A phrasal verb

(C) An idiom

(D) A preposition of place

(39) What does *every nook and cranny* mean?

(A) The most important places

(B) To the right audience

(C) Everywhere

(D) Among the elite

(40) What does *far-reaching* mean?

(A) To reach a lot of people

(B) To be influential

(C) To reach the right audience

(D) To be convincing

(41) What determines the potential impact of Facebook Ads on businesses?

(A) Facebook's billionaire owner

(B) Facebook's specially designed algorithm

(C) Facebook's huge number of active users

(D) All of the above

(42) Which feature of Facebook Ads allows videos to be used for promotion?

(A) Dynamic Ads

(B) Social Ads

(C) Visual Ads

(D) Audiovisual Ads

(43) Which of the following types of video is accepted for Facebook Ads?

(A) Long video

(B) Medium-length video

(C) Short video

(D) Video of any length

(44) Which of the following words can replace *undisputed* as used in the passage?

(A) Leading

(B) Frontrunner

(C) Irrefutable

(D) Unrecognized

(45) What is personalized content?

(A) Content created for each customer

(B) Content created for a specific group of customers

(C) Special content for holiday promos

(D) Content for Facebook users

(46) What should you bear in mind when creating promotional content for social media platforms?

(A) How to create the type of content that suits you

(B) How to create the type of content that suits each social media platform

(C) How to create general content for all social media platforms

(D) How to create as much content as possible

(47) Which of the following platforms depends on hashtags for promotion?

(A) Facebook

(B) Twitter

(C) None of the above

(D) A and B

(48) Differentiate between a business and a personal social media account.

(A) Personal accounts should be updated regularly, while business accounts should be updated occasionally.

(B) Business accounts should be updated once a year, while personal accounts should be updated occasionally.

(C) Personal accounts should be updated regularly, while business accounts may be updated occasionally.

(D) Business accounts should be updated regularly, while personal accounts may be updated occasionally.

(49) On what occasions should you consider updating your business social media accounts?

(A) When you have new products or services to promote

(B) When you are less busy

(C) Regularly

(D) Once a month

(50) Is there any danger in updating your business account only sporadically?

(A) No

(B) Yes

(C) Maybe

(D) Only in certain circumstances

(51) Why should you carefully study your competitors?

(A) To monitor their progress

(B) To learn from them

(C) To keep yourself busy

(D) To assist with promoting their goods or services

(52) When studying your competitors, what should you concentrate on?

(A) Their number of employees

(B) Their social media accounts

(C) What makes them stand out from the pack

(D) All of the above

(53) A *template* as used in the passage means what?

(A) A model

(B) A replica

(C) An imitation

(D) Something similar

(54) Why is regular interaction with your customers important?

(A) To keep both of you busy

(B) To build lasting business relationships

(C) To monitor their social media activities

(D) To stay abreast of the latest business news and information

(55) Which of the following should not be included in your online interactions with your customers?

(A) Local news and rumors

(B) Updates about your products or services

(C) Needs that your products or services can fill

(D) None of the above

(56) What word or phrase can replace *leveraged* as used in the passage?

(A) Took advantage of

(B) Considered irrelevant

(C) Studied the effects of

(D) Incorporated into your plans

Writing Test 2: Questions

(1) What are examples of indefinite pronouns?

(A) It, she, he and him

(B) It, she, herself and him

(C) We, she, he and him

(D) Everything, everyone, everybody and no one

(2) What are demonstrative pronouns used for?

(A) To demonstrate how pronouns are used

(B) To demonstrate the usefulness of nouns

(C) To replace nouns

(D) To highlight the importance of verbs

(3) Phrases and clauses should be connected to a noun or a pronoun with what pronoun type?

(A) Possessive pronoun

(B) Intensive pronoun

(C) Relative pronoun

(D) Connective pronoun

(4) *At sunrise, at noon* and *before sunrise* are examples of what?

(A) Adjectives

(B) Prepositional phrases used as adverbial phrases

(C) Prepositions of location

(D) Prepositional conjunctions

(5) Define *intensive pronoun.*

(A) A pronoun used for intensifying pronouns only

(B) A pronoun used for intensifying pronouns and nouns

(C) A pronoun used for intensifying pronouns and adjectives only

(D) A pronoun used for intensifying adverbs, nouns and pronouns

(6) "He bought a new home a month after replacing his vehicle." What preposition is expressed in this sentence?

(A) Preposition of agency

(B) Prepositional condition

(C) Preposition of time

(D) Preposition of instrument

(7) Which of the following is not a type of preposition?

(A) Preposition of agent

(B) Preposition of time

(C) Preposition of condition

(D) Preposition of direction

(8) Define *preposition of instrument.*

(A) A type of preposition used for devices, instruments and machines

(B) A type of preposition used for devices, instruments and ammunition

(C) A type of preposition used for ammunition, instruments and weapons

(D) A type of preposition used for devices, instruments, weapons and machines

(9) Define *preposition of place.*

(A) Used for addressing the specific location of an item, person or object

(B) Used for addressing the specific location of people in relation to time and place

(C) Used for addressing the specific location of an item, person or object in relation to the object's environment

(D) Used for addressing the specific location of an item, person or object for research and academic purposes

(10) "The book is written by a renowned writer." What type of preposition is used in the sentence?

(A) Preposition of transportation

(B) Preposition of agent

(C) Preposition of place

(D) Preposition of relationship

(11) Differentiate between *in* and *at*.

(A) *In* defines specific places, while *at* defines physical or virtual boundaries

(B) *In* defines random places, while *at* defines physical or virtual boundaries

(C) *At* defines specific places, while *in* defines physical or virtual boundaries

(D) *At* defines random places, while *in* defines physical or virtual boundaries

(12) When is *on* used?

(A) To define the relationship between objects or things in relation to their surfaces

(B) To define the relationship between objects based on color

(C) To define the relationship between multiple objects based on mass

(D) To define the relationship between two objects or things in relation to their location

(13) What are the two classes of action verbs?

(A) Transitive and intransitive

(B) Transitive and untransitive

(C) Primary and intransitive

(D) Transitive and primary

(14) When is a preposition of time used?

(A) To indicate the time something happened in the past

(B) To indicate the time something happened in the future

(C) To indicate the time something happened in the night

(D) To indicate the time of occurrence of something in general

(15) What is the adverb of frequency in "He often leaves home before dawn"?

(A) Before

(B) Often

(C) Leaves

(D) Dawn

(16) The causal relationship between verbs and nouns is best expressed with what type of preposition?

(A) Preposition of relationship

(B) Preposition of agent

(C) Preposition of instrument

(D) Preposition of connection

(17) *By*, *with*, *on* and *with* are examples of what type of preposition?

(A) Preposition of connection

(B) Preposition of instrument

(C) Preposition of documentation

(D) Preposition of direction

(18) "I will pass through the subway on my way home" uses what type of preposition?

(A) Preposition of instrument

(B) Preposition of agent

(C) Preposition of direction

(D) Preposition of frequency

(19) Which of the following contains an intransitive verb?

(A) He likes reading books.

(B) He plays football.

(C) She dances well.

(D) I am watching soccer.

(20) Differentiate between an intransitive and a transitive verb.

(A) An intransitive verb requires an object, but a transitive verb does not.

(B) A transitive verb requires an object, but an intransitive verb does not.

(C) An intransitive verb requires a subject, but a transitive verb does not.

(D) An intransitive verb requires an object and a subject, but a transitive verb does not.

(21) Which of the following sentences contains an adverb of frequency?

(A) He hardly stays indoors on weekends.

(B) She was gorgeous.

(C) That is worrisome.

(D) None of the above.

(22) What are auxiliary verbs?

(A) Verbs that express emotions and feelings

(B) Verbs that express emotions and emphasis

(C) Verbs that express modality and emphasis

(D) Verbs that express modality and feelings

(23) Define *regular verbs*.

(A) Verbs that are regularly used in sentences

(B) Verbs that are randomly used in sentences

(C) Verbs that form tenses by following an established pattern

(D) Verbs that form tenses with pronouns

(24) Which of the following are all irregular verbs?

(A) Go, drink, come and write

(B) Busy, bury, sleep and walk

(C) Work, dance, sing and play

(D) Sing, walk, busy and play

(25) Adverbs are generally known as what?

(A) Adverbs, adjectives or adverb modifiers

(B) Adverbs, conjunctions or adverb modifiers

(C) Adverbs, adjectives or adverb qualifiers

(D) Adverbs, adjectives or adverb modifiers and qualifiers

(26) What is the purpose of an adverb of time in a sentence?

(A) It determines how fast the action occurs.

(B) It shows the time lapse between two actions.

(C) It determines the urgency of the time information provided by the adverb.

(D) It determines the urgency of the usefulness of the information provided by the adverb.

(27) What are adverbs of degree?

(A) Adverbs that define the degree of occurrence of an event

(B) Adverbs that express the intensity of the adjective or adverb

(C) Adverbs that express the degree of an accident or an event

(D) Adverbs that show how quickly an event occurs

(28) What is the adverb of manner in “She could play soccer with ease”?

(A) Play

(B) Could

(C) With ease

(D) None of the above

(29) Correct this sentence: “This is my mothers pair of shoes.”

(A) This is my mothers pair of shoes.

(B) This is my mothers’ pair of shoes.

(C) This is my mother’s pair of shoes.

(D) This is my mothers’ pairs’ of shoes.

(30) *Fortnightly*, *annually* and *never* are examples of what part of speech?

(A) Adverbs of time

(B) Prepositions of time

(C) Prepositions of instrument

(D) Adverbs of condition

(31) *Sometimes, seldom* and *always* are examples of what type of adverb?

(A) Adverbs of frequency

(B) Adverbs of manner

(C) Adverbs of emergency

(D) Adverbs of time

(32) What are interjections used for?

(A) To express satisfaction

(B) To express personal conviction

(C) To express both simple and complex ideas

(D) To express sudden emotions and strong feelings

(33) Clauses and phrases are connected by what part of speech?

(A) Interjections

(B) Exclamations

(C) Conjunctions

(D) Adverbial clauses of connection

(34) Under what condition are subordinating conjunctions used?

(A) To connect two clauses with identical grammatical values

(B) To connect multiple clauses with identical grammatical values

(C) To connect two clauses with different grammatical values

(D) To connect multiple clauses with different grammatical values

(35) *But, for, nor* and *or* are examples of what type of conjunction?

(A) Adverbial

(B) Correlative

(C) Coordinating

(D) Subordinating

(36) Which of the following pairs is not a type of conjunction?

(A) Subordinating conjunctions and coordinating conjunctions

(B) Correlative conjunctions and adverbial conjunctions

(C) Subordinating and coordinating conjunctions

(D) Coordinating and coordinate conjunctions

(37) Differentiate between adverbs of manner and adverbs of frequency.

(A) Adverbs of frequency show how something is done, while adverbs of manner refer to how often an event occurs

(B) Adverbs of manner show how people react to problems, while adverbs of frequency refer to how often an event occurs

(C) Adverbs of manner show how something is done, while adverbs of frequency refer to how often an event occurs

(D) Adverbs of manner show how something is done, while adverbs of frequency refer to the degree at which something is done

(38) *Arrogantly*, *quickly*, *suddenly* and *beautifully* are examples of what type of adverb?

(A) Adverbs of time

(B) Adverbs of condition

(C) Adverbs of frequency

(D) Adverbs of manner

(39) Which of the following contains a transitive verb?

(A) She walks slowly.

(B) He plays football after school.

(C) She can sleep for hours.

(D) It is neither here nor there.

(40) What punctuation mark is missing in "What a miss"?

(A) Interjection

(B) Exclamation

(C) Preposition

(D) Apostrophe

Essay 3: Is Technology Beneficial for the Education System?

Technology, with its astonishing impact on people, has come to stay. The classroom has not been spared the huge effect of innovation. In recent years, chalkboards have been replaced by whiteboards and markers, and students can do research from the comfort of home thanks to search engines such as Google. However, is technological advancement beneficial or detrimental to the education system?

In some quarters, the argument is that technology has produced a generation of lazy students who are spoon-fed by the search engines mentioned above. The use of modern technology for criminal activities is another argument. Some people are also of the opinion that students are distracted by technology. Nevertheless, a look at some outstanding benefits of technology shows that its benefits for learning far outweigh its side effects.

Technology has proven over the years to encourage individual learning. This is a positive for the proponents of technology in the classroom, considering that students have different learning rates and abilities. Students can take advantage of technological resources to learn at their own pace.

Physically challenged or struggling students can also benefit from the learning opportunities provided by the latest technology, using the vast quantities of resources at their disposal to minimize their disabilities and improve their academic performance.

Modern learning is not all about reading and writing. It also includes learning important skills that enhance students' marketability in the future. Thus, they must learn critical thinking skills, complex problem-solving skills, leadership skills and other important skills. These skills are best learned in collaboration with others.

Students can also leverage the power of technology to collaborate with their classmates who are separated from them during global crises or natural disasters. A typical example of such technology is Zoom, a fast-rising communication app that enables people to communicate irrespective of their geographical locations in the world.

Improved engagement is another important benefit of technology in the education system. When students are taught through games or are taken on virtual teaching-based trips, they are more engaged in such lessons. The engagement will improve their retention of key information, as well as their overall performance in the classroom.

Technology keeps evolving. Innovations from a mere decade or two ago have already become obsolete. Thus, to keep abreast of current events in the world in preparation for the future, it is imperative that students be allowed to learn as much as they can about technology and use it extensively for their academic work. This will prepare them for the future, as they will be able to easily adapt to changes in technology and jobs.

Essay 3 Questions

(1) What has changed about modern learning?

(A) Nothing

(B) The learning process and techniques

(C) The level of interest

(D) None of the above

(2) Why is it necessary to keep up with new technology?

(A) To while away time

(B) To prove your versatility

(C) To remain relevant in your career

(D) All of the above

Essay 4: Should Male Workers Be Given Paternity Leave?

For centuries in the United States, new dads did not give a second thought to paternity leave because it was considered the prerogative of new moms. Today, though, new dads are also pushing for paid paternity leave. Is that a smart move? Should companies give their male employees paternity leave?

The proponents of paid paternity leave for dads base their request on the multiple benefits of granting new fathers the opportunity to stay home from work for a defined period of time. According to people of this mindset, if both parents are granted parental leave, it offers them the opportunity to coparent the new addition to their family. Couples will thus benefit from the arrangement if both parents are able to take their parental leave simultaneously.

Presently, there is a societal perception that caring for newborns is an exclusively female responsibility. This mindset is behind some men's negative attitude toward caring for their new babies. But if new dads are given paternity leave, more men will be involved in taking care of their young children. This will change the negative narrative and make caregiving a lot more attractive for men. As an increasing number of men take up the responsibility, new mothers can take a deserved rest.

Paternity leave also allows fathers to bond with their new babies. When fathers take care of their babies by feeding and diapering them, they will build a good relationship with them. According to studies published by the *New York Times*, fathers who are granted two weeks or more of paternity leave are more likely to continue taking care of their babies after that leave is over than fathers who are not there from the beginning.

In 2016, Chris Fabro, the global head of compensation and benefits at Bank of America, noted that the bank experienced unprecedented employee satisfaction when parental leave for its employees was increased from 12 to 16 weeks. As a result, employee retention increased. If the policy is extended to all sectors of the US economy, a profound positive impact can be anticipated.

Opponents of paternity talk about the stigmatization fathers may experience at work or elsewhere, as they may be seen as not giving their all to their job. Nevertheless, the government should lay a good foundation for father-child bonding, encourage more fathers to see paternity leave in a positive light and help eliminate the unfortunate stigma attached to this idea.

Essay 4 Questions

(1) Why are most dads pushing for paternity leave?

(A) For their own selfish interests

(B) To enable them to support their wives and new babies

(C) To cut down on work-related expenses

(D) To garner public sympathy

(2) Why are some men against paternity leave?

(A) Many men are scared of their wives.

(B) They are scared of a backlash from people.

(C) They are not interested in their new babies.

(D) They want extra income.

Mathematics Test 2: Answers & Explanations

(1) (C) 5/6 and 10/12.

To test the equivalency of two ratios, convert them to decimals and compare their values. The same values mean equivalency. 5/6 and 10/12 are both 0.8333333.

(2) (B) 15/21.

To determine the equivalent ratio, identify the ratio with the same decimal value as 5/7.

(3) (C) 4/5.

Both 16 and 20 are multiples of 4. So, divide through by 4. Then, you have (16/4)/(20/4) = 4/5. Thus, 16/20 = 4/5 in the lowest terms.

(4) (C) 1:2.

Both 21 and 42 are multiples of 3, 7 and 21. Divide through by 21 and get 1:2. If you are not sure, start with 3 and keep dividing until you are done.

(5) (C) 1/3.

Total income = $150

Expenses on food and gas = $50

Ratio of income to expenses is $150:$50. Divide through by $50.

$150:$50 = $150/$50: $50/$50 = 3:1.

Therefore, the ratio of the man's income to his expenses is 3:1.

(6) (C) 1/2.

Total distance = 100 miles

Distance completed = 50 miles

Distance completed = total distance = 50 miles:100 miles

Divide through by 50 miles = 1/2.

(7) (A) 1/3.

Number of parts = 3

Number of parts completed = 2

Number of parts left = 3 − 2 = 1

Number left = number of parts = 1/3.

(8) (C) By cross-multiplying the two values.

To determine the proportionality of two values, cross-multiply them. If one side of the equation equals the other side, the two values are equal.

(9) (A) They are proportional.

2:3 = 14:21. To cross-multiply, multiply 3 by 14 and 1 by 21.

3 * 14 = 42. 21 * 1 = 21. Thus, they are proportional.

(10) (B) 14.

2/3 = x:21

For equality, 3 * x = 2 * 21

3x = 42

Divide through by 3.

x = 14.

(11) (C) 2.

y/3 = 24/36

For proportionality, 3 * 24 = y * 36

72 = 36y

Divide through by 36.

y = 2.

(12) (C) 60 expressed with respect to 100.

When numbers are expressed as a percentage, they are expressed in relation to 100. When you see expressions like 60%, it means 60 out of 100.

(13) (A) 66.7%.

Number of passengers = 60

Number of female passengers = 20

Number of male passengers = 60 – 20 = 40 passengers

Male passengers as a percentage of total number of passengers = (40/60) * 100

= 0.667 * 100 = 66.7%.

(14) (D) 75%.

Convert 15/20 to a decimal and multiply the result by 100. Alternatively, (15/20) * 100 = 1,500/20. Either way, the result is 75%.

(15) (D) 60%.

Divide 12 by 20 and multiply the result by 100.

12/20 = 0.6

0.6 * 100 = 60

Hence, 12 is 60% of 20.

(16) (C) 1 meter = 100 centimeters.

There are 100 centimeters in 1 meter.

(17) (A) 932 miles.

1 kilometer = 0.6214 miles

1,500 kilometers = (1,500 * 0.6214) miles

Thus, 1,500 = 932.1 miles, or approximately 932 miles.

(18) (B) 236 kilograms.

2.2046 pounds = 1 kilogram

520 pounds = (520/2.2046) kilograms

Thus, 520 pounds = 235.9 kilograms, or approximately 236 kilograms.

(19) (B) 1,524 centimeters.

1 foot = 30.48 centimeters

50 feet = (50 * 30.48) centimeters

50 feet = 1,524 centimeters.

(20) (A) 9.3 square meters.

1 square meter = 10.76 square feet

100 square feet = (100/10.76) square meters = 9.29 square meters.

(21) (A) 1,931 kilometers.

1 mile = 1.609 kilometers

1,200 miles = (1,200 * 1.609) kilometers = 1,930.8, or approximately 1,931 kilometers.

(22) (D) 17,637 pounds.

Vehicle's weight = 8,000 kilograms

1 kilogram = 2.2046 pounds

Thus, 8,000 kilograms = 8,000 * 2.2046 pounds = 17,636.8 pounds.

(23) (B) 1,570.

Since the last digit is 7, it will be rounded up and added to the next figure, 6, and becomes 7. Hence, 1,567 is 1,570 to the nearest 10.

(24) (D) 12,300.

The last two digits are 45. Since it is not up to 50, it will be rounded down to 0. Hence, 12,345 is 12,300 to the nearest hundred.

(25) (A) 5,600.

Since the last two digits are 27 and not up to 50, it will be rounded down to 0. Hence, 5,627 is 5,600 to the nearest hundred.

(26) (C) 56.2.

The last digit is 3, which is less than 5. Hence, it will be rounded down to 0. Therefore, 56.23 is 56.2 to the nearest tenth.

(27) (C) 234.57.

The next digits after two decimal places are 678. Rounding up from the right, you get 700. Thus, 234.5678 is 234.57 to two decimal places.

(28) (A) 267.0.

After the three digits, you have .23. Since 23 is less than 50, it is rounded down. Hence, 267.23 is 267.0 to three significant figures.

(29) (D) 0.0046.

After the first two significant figures, round the next digits down or up as required. Hence, 0.0045678 is 0.0046 to two significant figures.

(30) (C) Corresponding values and coefficients.

Some common terms in algebra include coefficients, like terms and unlike terms. Corresponding values are not a term in algebra.

(31) (A) Algebraic expressions with the same variables and exponents.

Like terms are algebraic expressions with the same variables and exponents, while unlike terms are expressions whose variables or exponents are different.

(32) (C) 5ab + 5xy.

2ab + 4xy + xy + 3ab

Organize the like terms.

= 2ab + 3ab + 4xy + xy = 5ab + 5xy.

(33) (A) 8bc + 8cd +5ay + 2xy.

For 5bc + 8 cd + 3ay +3bc + 2ay + 2xy, organize the like terms.

5bc + 8 cd + 3ay +3bc + 2ay + 2xy = 5bc + 3bc +8cd + 3ay + 2ay + 2xy

= 8bc +8cd + 5ay + 2xy.

(34) (A) 6ab + 3bc + 6xy.

To simplify 8ab + 3bc + 10xy – 2ab -4xy, organize the like terms.

= 8ab – 2ab + 3bc + 10xy – 4xy = 6ab + 3bc + 6xy.

(35) (D) 5ab + 4cd.

(10ab + 8cd) – (5ab + 4cd)

Open the parentheses.

10ab – 5ab + 8cd – 4cd = 5ab + 4cd.

(36) (C) 9a.

To divide 45ab by 5b, divide 45 by 5 and ab by b.

45/5 = 9, ab/b = a. Thus, 45ab divided by 5b = 9a.

(37) (D) 3b.

To divide $36b^2$ by 12b, divide 36 by 12 and b^2 by b.

$36/12 = 3$

$b^2/b = (b * b)/b = b$

Therefore, $36b^2$ divided by 12b = 3b.

(38) (C) $a^2 + 5a + 6$.

$(a + 2) * (a + 3) = a (a + 3) + 2 (a + 3)$

$= (a^2 + 3a) + (2a + 6)$

$= a^2 + 3a + 2a + 6$

$= a^2 + 5a + 6$.

(39) (B) $a^2 + 7a + 12$.

$(a + 4) * (a + 3) = a (a + 3) + 4(a + 3)$

$= (a^2 + 3a) + (4a – 12)$

$= a^2 + 3a + 4a – 12$

$= a^2 +7a + 12$.

(40) (D) Shapes that have two measurable dimensions—the length and the width.

Two-dimensional shapes are shapes that have two measurable dimensions, namely the length and the width.

(41) (A) Sphere, cuboid and circle.

Some examples of two-dimensional shapes are circles, squares, quadrilaterals, triangles, rectangles and pentagons. Cuboids and spheres are not two-dimensional.

(42) (B) A geometrical shape with four right angles and four equal sides.

A square is a geometrical shape with four right angles, four equal sides and four lines of symmetry.

(43) (D) The opposite angles are right angles.

The opposite sides of a rhombus are parallel (not right angles), while all four sides are equal in size. Rhombuses have two lines of symmetry, which can be four lines if the rhombus is a square.

(44) (A) Rectangles, rhombuses and trapezoids.

Some examples of quadrilaterals are squares, rectangles, parallelograms, rhombuses, kites, trapezoids and others. Circles and cylinders are not quadrilaterals.

(45) (D) Acute and octane.

There arc different types of triangles. These include scalene, obtuse, equilateral, isosceles right-angle and acute.

(46) (C) A triangle with one angle greater than 90 degrees.

Obtuse triangles have one angle that is greater than 90 degrees. The other two angles are acute, or less than 90 degrees.

(47) (B) 180 degrees.

Irrespective of the type of triangle, the sum of the angles of a triangle is 180 degrees, or two right angles.

(48) (A) An isosceles triangle has two equal sides and angles, while one of the angles of a right-angle triangle is 90 degrees.

Two angles and sides of an isosceles triangle are equal. On the other hand, one of the angles of a right-angle triangle is 90 degrees.

(49) (B) The square of the hypotenuse side of a right triangle is equal to the sum of the squares of the other sides of the triangle.

The Pythagorean Theorem states that the square of the hypotenuse side of a right triangle is equal to the sum of the squares of the other sides of the triangle.

(50) (C) The hypotenuse.

The longest side of a right triangle is the hypotenuse. It is opposite the triangle's 90-degree angle.

(51) (B) 5 cm.

Base a = 3 cm

Perpendicular b = 4 cm

Hypotenuse $c = \sqrt{(a^2 + b^2)} = \sqrt{(3^2 + 4^2)}$

$= \sqrt{(9 + 16)} = \sqrt{25} = 5$.

(52) (A) 6 cm.

Hypotenuse a = 10 cm

Base b = 8 cm

Opposite is given by $c = \sqrt{a^2 - b^2}$

$= \sqrt{10^2 - 8^2} = \sqrt{100 - 64}$

$= \sqrt{36} = 6.$

(53) (C) 6.25 cm.

Base a = 5 cm

Hypotenuse b = 8 cm

Perpendicular c is given by $c = \sqrt{b^2 - a^2}$

$= \sqrt{8^2 - 5^2} = \sqrt{64 - 25}$

$= \sqrt{39} = 6.2449s.$

(54) (A) $c^2 = a^2 + b^2$.

A Pythagorean triple is a type of right triangle with all positive sides such that the sides obey the formula $c^2 = a^2 + b^2$.

(55) (A) 3, 4 and 5.

Some examples of Pythagorean triples are:

3, 4, 5

5, 12, 13

6, 8, 10

8, 15, 17.

(56) (D) Pentagons and hexagons.

Polygons are named by their number of sides. Pentagons and hexagons are five-sided and six-sided polygons, respectively.

Reading Test 2: Answers & Explanations

(1) (A) A period of time when technology is extensively used.

The digital age, i.e., today, is a period of time when people are using technology extensively.

(2) (D) Business people.

Entrepreneurs are business people. They run their own businesses, unlike people working in the corporate world.

(3) (C) And so on.

What have you means *and so on*. It is used to indicate that there is more to a certain list. i.e., "I bought apples, oranges, grapes *and so on*" would imply the person bought other types of fruit.

(4) (D) Skype.

Facebook, Twitter and other websites are resources you can use to give your business an online presence. However, Skype is an online communication application that is not specifically designed for business promotion.

(5) (A) Limited customer base.

Keeping your business offline limits your customer base to your immediate environment. When you take your business online, you can overcome this challenge and promote your brand to the world.

(6) (D) No off time.

A business that is promoted over the internet allows for a 24/7 presence. Customers may order your goods and services at any hour of the day, even when you are asleep.

(7) (B) You have a global market to explore.

The biggest benefit of promoting your business online is that you have the entire world as your marketplace to explore.

(8) (A) By communicating regularly with your customers.

Regular communication is the key to building a lasting business relationship with your customers, especially if you are promoting your business online.

(9) (A) Promoting your business to make it attractive to potential and existing customers.

Branding is the practice of promoting your business to increase its appeal to potential and existing customers.

(10) (A) It enables people to identify your business.

Since you are not the only one in your line of business, you may be lost in the crowd if you do not clearly brand your products or services. Branding allows people to easily identify your business as it stands out from the crowd.

(11) (B) With strong competition.

When something is competitive, it can stand up to the others in the market. In the business world, entrepreneurs in the same line of business compete for the same audience. That makes it a competitive marketplace.

(12) (B) Being better than your competitors.

When you stand out, you are different from and better than others. In the business world, it means you are better than your competitors.

(13) (C) Being in a better position.

When you have an edge over someone or something, it means you have an advantage of some kind.

(14) (D) A and B.

When you are too far away from your customers, communication becomes a lot more difficult. This means your customers may look for more convenient alternatives.

(15) (D) A and B.

By sharing valuable tips with your customers and getting to know them better, you can develop and sustain their interest in your brand.

(16) (B) You deal with your customers as humans, not just as a source of income.

When you bring a human dimension to your business, you treat your customers as people, not just as money-generating machines.

(17) (A) The practice is outdated.

It means that limiting one's business to one's immediate environment was the norm but has been outdated by technology that allows businesses to now be promoted worldwide.

(18) (C) In other words.

Conversely means *in other words*. It can also mean the *opposite of something*.

(19) (B) Not working for a particular employer.

When you freelance, you sell your services to multiple organizations rather than being on a single organization's payroll.

(20) (C) Because of the proliferation of websites.

The increasing number of websites has also called for an increasing number of skilled writers. Hence, freelance writers seize the opportunity to work for multiple organizations simultaneously.

(21) (B) Enjoying abundant opportunities.

When you have a field day, you enjoy what you are doing. Freelancers cherish the abundant opportunities they have.

(22) (C) Idiomatic.

When you "work behind the scenes," it means that you are doing something in a way that people are not aware of. The phrase is an idiom.

(23) (D) None of the above.

Freelancers are needed to write articles and other materials for podcasts, YouTube channels, blogs, magazines and websites. They also write eBooks, assist with dissertations and more.

(24) (C) For branding.

Businesses create logos as part of their branding efforts. Together with websites, businesses use logos to create unique identities to distinguish themselves from their competitors.

(25) (B) Availability and skill levels.

A logo designer must be available to meet customers' requests. The designer's skill level will also help determine his or her success in the field.

(26) (D) None of the above.

Businesses create logos for souvenirs, video animation, GIFs, websites and social media assets. These are some of the ways they promote their brands.

(27) (C) There is an increasing number of websites.

With millions of websites hosted on the internet, website designers are in high demand.

(28) (B) For promotional purposes.

Businesses are creating websites to promote their products and make them readily available to potential customers in any part of the world.

(29) (C) Personalized logos.

Trademarked logos are personalized and cannot be used by any other brand without copyright permission. For instance, Nike and Coca-Cola have trademarked logos that were designed solely for their use.

(30) (A) It allows you to work at your own pace and convenience.

Since you are working from the comfort of your home and are not contracted to any one employer, you can work at your own convenience and pace as a freelancer.

(31) (C) To help them promote their businesses on social media platforms.

Businesses hire social media marketers to help them promote their businesses on social media platforms such as Facebook, Instagram and Twitter.

(32) (D) Never.

Freelancing existed well before the internet and will continue to exist for many decades. This is the prediction of economists and government leaders.

(33) (C) Skills.

This is a no-brainer. If you are contemplating joining the freelancing industry, the most important factor you should consider is your skills. For instance, if you are a good writer with zero design skills, it is a waste of your time and resources to try and become a freelance graphic designer.

(34) (B) Another source of income aside from your regular job.

Your side hustle is another source of income you create to supplement your regular income.

(35) (D) People with the required skills.

If you lack any skills you can monetize as a freelancer, you should consider a different kind of work. You must have key skills to be a successful freelancer, as discussed in the passage.

(36) (C) Corporate job.

In the corporate world, employees generally work from 9:00 a.m. to 5:00 p.m., Monday to Friday. Hence, such jobs are referred to as nine-to-five jobs.

(37) (D) A and B.

From the passage, it is clear that people with the required skill sets can join the freelancing world. Thus, people who have skills they can monetize can beat unemployment by monetizing their skills as freelancers.

(38) (C) An idiom.

Every nook and cranny is an idiom. Hyperbole is an exaggeration, while phrasal verbs and prepositions of place are other types of expression entirely.

(39) (C) Everywhere.

As an idiom, *every nook and cranny* refers to every aspect of a situation or every part of a place. Contextually, it can mean *everywhere.*

(40) (B) To be influential.

Far-reaching means *likely to have many effects or a lot of influence.*

(41) (C) Facebook's huge number of active users.

Facebook has over a billion active daily users. Thus, Facebook Ads can reach a wide audience, depending on your target audience and product or services.

(42) (A) Dynamic Ads.

With Facebook's Dynamic Ads, you can use videos to deliver personalized advertising to prospective consumers. This is a special Facebook feature designed for video-based ads.

(43) (C) Short videos.

You can reach your target audience and create more impact by including short promotional videos to boost your Facebook Ads conversion.

(44) (C) Irrefutable.

Irrefutable can replace *undisputed* as used in the passage because they are synonyms. Both words mean *cannot be proven wrong*.

(45) (B) Content created for a specific group of customers.

Personalized content is created for a specific group of customers. For instance, if a company promotes health and wellness products, it cannot use the same promotional content for both pregnant women and senior citizens.

(46) (B) How to create the type of content that suits each social media platform.

You should always bear in mind that each social media platform has unique features. For instance, Facebook allows users to create content of any length. On Twitter, you are limited to 160 characters. Understanding this will guide you when creating content for such platforms.

(47) (B) Twitter.

Twitter depends on hashtags for promotion. Facebook users can decide whether to use hashtags or not. Instagram is another social media platform that uses hashtags extensively.

(48) (D) Business accounts should be updated regularly, while personal accounts may be updated occasionally.

A major distinction between your personal social media account and a business account is that while you may update the former at your convenience, you must update the latter regularly.

(49) (C) Regularly.

You should update your social media accounts regularly, whether you have new products to promote or not. This is because regular updates show your customers that you are still active in business and are always available for them.

(50) (B) Yes.

Updating your business account erratically will cause you to lose customers. Some may mistake your inactivity to mean you are out of business. Others may think you just don't care about your customers any longer.

(51) (B) To learn from them.

Monitoring your competition allows you to learn from their successes and errors.

(52) (C) What makes them stand out from the pack.

If your competitors are better than you, find out what gives them an edge over you and try to imitate them. Learn their tricks and apply them to grow your own business.

(53) (A) A model.

As used in the passage, a *template* is a model. It describes something you can replicate for your own business and audience.

(54) (B) To build lasting business relationships.

Just as regular communication with your friends keeps your relationships alive, regular interactions with your customers will help you to build lasting business relationships.

(55) (A) Local news and rumors.

Unless local news and rumors have an impact on your business, your interactions with your customers or clients should be devoid of such topics. Stick to updates about your brands and needs you can fulfill for your audience.

(56) (A) Took advantage of.

Leveraged, as used in the passage, means *took advantage of*. This implies that you can seize an opportunity to grow your business.

Writing Test 2: Answers & Explanations

(1) (D) Everything, everyone, everybody and no one.

Indefinite pronouns include *everything, everyone, everybody, no one* and others. These pronouns do not refer to a specific noun.

(2) (C) To replace nouns.

Demonstrative pronouns replace nouns. Sometimes, when such pronouns perform the roles of demonstrative adjectives, they modify nouns or pronouns.

(3) (A) Possessive pronoun.

Possessive pronouns are used to connected phrases and clauses.

(4) (B) Prepositional phrases used as adverbial phrases.

At sunrise, at noon and *before sunrise* are some examples of prepositional phrases used as adverbial phrases. They are used to specify when an event occurred, will occur or is now occurring.

(5) (B) A pronoun used for intensifying pronouns and nouns.

Intensive pronouns are used to intensify nouns or pronouns. They come after the pronoun or noun they intensify in a sentence.

(6) (C) Preposition of time.

A month after indicates the specific time the event occurred. Thus, it is a preposition of time.

(7) (C) Preposition of condition.

A preposition of condition is not a type of preposition. The different types of prepositions are prepositions of direction, prepositions of time, prepositions of agent, prepositions of instrument and prepositions of place.

(8) (A) A type of preposition used for devices, instruments and machines.

A preposition of instrument is used for an array of instruments, devices or machines. Examples of such prepositions are *with*, *by*, *on* and *with the help of*.

(9) (A) Used for addressing the specific location of an item, person or object.

A preposition of place is used for addressing the specific location of a person, object or item.

(10) (B) Preposition of agent.

The *by* in the sentence is a preposition of agent. The causal relationships between verbs and nouns are expressed with prepositions of agent.

(11) (C) *At* defines specific places, while *in* defines physical or virtual boundaries.

At is a preposition of place. *In* is a preposition of direction.

(12) (A) To define the relationship between objects or things in relation to their surfaces.

When defining the relationship between two objects or things in relation to their surfaces, *on* is used.

(13) (A) Transitive and intransitive.

Action verbs are classified into intransitive and transitive verbs, each with distinct attributes and uses.

(14) (D) To indicate the time something occurred in the present.

A preposition of time is useful when indicating when something will occur in general, whether the future, past, present, etc.

(15) (B) Often.

Often shows how frequently he leaves home before dawn. Thus, it is an adverb of frequency.

(16) (B) Preposition of agent.

A preposition of agent is used to express the causal relationship between nouns and verbs.

(17) (B) Preposition of instrument.

A preposition of instrument can be used for instruments, devices or machines, but is not limited to just these things. *With*, *by* and *on* are some examples.

(18) (C) Preposition of direction.

This class of preposition is specifically designed for direction indication.

(19) (C) She dances well.

Intransitive verbs do not have an object for the verb. "I am watching soccer" contains an object, which is "soccer." The other options also have objects for the verbs mentioned in the sentences. "Well" is not an object.

(20) (B) A transitive verb requires an object, but an intransitive verb does not.

The major difference between an intransitive verb and a transitive verb is that while the former does not require an object, the latter does.

(21) (A) He hardly stays indoors on weekends.

"He hardly stays indoors on weekends" contains an adverb of frequency, *hardly*.

(22) (C) Verbs that express modality and emphasis.

Auxiliary verbs are used for expressing concepts such as modality and emphasis.

(23) (C) Verbs that form tenses by following an established pattern.

Regular verbs form their tenses by following an established pattern. Some examples of such verbs are *bury* and *create*.

(24) (A) Go, drink, come and write.

Go, *drink*, *come* and *write* is a set of irregular verbs. These verbs do not follow an established pattern when forming the past tense and past participle.

(25) (A) Adverb, adjectives or adverb modifiers.

Adverbs are used for describing or modifying another adverb, adjective, verb or a group of words. They are also extensively used to modify clauses, sentences, determiners and prepositions.

(26) (C) It determines the urgency of the time information provided by the adverb.

An adverb of time determines the urgency of the time information in the sentence.

(27) (B) Adverbs that express the intensity of the adjective or adverb.

The intensity of the level of adjective or adverb used in a sentence is expressed with an adjective of degree. These adverbs modify the adjective, noun or adverb they precede in a sentence.

(28) (C) With ease.

With ease is an adverb of manner in the sentence. It shows the subject's manner of playing soccer.

(29) (C) This is my mother's pair of shoes.

This sentence correctly uses an apostrophe to show possession. The apostrophe comes before the *s*, indicating just one mother owns the shoes.

(30) (A) Adverbs of time.

Annually, *fortnightly* and *never* are examples of adverbs of time. They indicate the time an event occurs.

(31) (A) Adverbs of frequency.

The frequency of the occurrence of an action is expressed with an adverb of frequency. *Always*, *sometimes*, *seldom* and *rarely* are some examples of such adverbs.

(32) (D) To express sudden emotions and strong feelings.

Sudden emotions and strong feelings are usually expressed with interjections. Some strong emotions that can be expressed with interjections are happiness, sadness, shock and excitement.

(33) (C) Conjunctions.

Conjunctions are words that connect multiple words, clauses or phrases.

(34) (C) To connect two clauses with different grammatical values.

When two clauses have different grammatical values, they are best connected with subordinating conjunctions, such as *so that, unless, when, how* and *after.*

(35) (C) Coordinating.

Examples of this type of conjunction include *but, or, nor, so* and *for.*

(36) (D) Coordinating and coordinate conjunctions.

Conjunctions are classified into subordinating, coordinating, adverbial and correlative. Thus, coordinate conjunctions do not exist.

(37) (C) Adverbs of manner show how something is done, while adverbs of frequency refer to how often an event occurs.

Adverbs of manner show how something is done, while adverbs of frequency show an event's frequency of occurrence.

(38) (D) Adverbs of manner.

Adverbs of manner end with *-ly*. *Quickly, arrogantly, beautifully, slowly* and *suddenly* are some examples of adverbs of manner.

(39) (B) He plays football after school.

Because the verb *plays* requires an object, *football,* it is a transitive verb.

(40) (A) Interjection.

A strong emotion is expressed in the sentence, thereby requiring an exclamatory mark.

Essay 3 Answers & Explanations

(1) (B) The learning process and techniques.

Modern learning is not all about reading and writing. It also includes learning important skills that will enhance students' marketability in the future.

(2) (C) To remain relevant in your career.

The evolution of technology is so rapid that "new" technology swiftly becomes obsolete. Thus, to remain relevant in your career, it is important to embrace technological innovations.

Essay 4 Answers & Explanations

(1) (B) To enable them to support their wives and new babies.

If new dads are given paternity leave, more men will be involved in taking care of their young children.

(2) (B) They are scared of a backlash from people.

The opponents of paternity leave talk about the stigmatization such fathers may experience at work or elsewhere. Men who take such leave could be construed as not giving their all to their careers.

Mathematics Test 3: Questions

(1) How are geometric shapes formed?

(A) By the closure of a shape's angles

(B) By the closure of a shape's curves, points and lines

(C) By the closure of a shape's angles and sides

(D) By the closure of a shape's diagonals and angles

(2) What are the types of geometric shapes?

(A) Simple and complex

(B) Three-dimensional and four-dimensional

(C) Two-dimensional and three-dimensional

(D) Primary and secondary

(3) What is the perimeter of a square with 7 cm sides?

(A) 21 cm

(B) 14 cm

(C) 35 cm

(D) 28 cm

(4) What is the length of a square if the perimeter of the square is 60 cm?

(A) 12 cm

(B) 20 cm

(C) 15 cm

(D) 25 cm

(5) What is the area of a square with 10 cm sides?

(A) 20 cm^2

(B) 100 cm

(C) 20 cm

(D) 100 cm^2

(6) If the area of a square is 225 cm^2, what is the length of each side?

(A) 20 cm

(B) 12 cm

(C) 15 cm

(D) 13 cm

(7) What is the perimeter of a triangle with sides that measure 6 cm, 8 cm and 12 cm?

(A) 13 cm

(B) 24 cm

(C) 26 cm

(D) 30 cm

(8) Find the perimeter of a triangle with sides that measure 3 cm, 7 cm and 8 cm.

(A) 15 cm

(B) 18 cm

(C) 6 cm

(D) 20 cm

(9) If the perimeter of an equilateral triangle is 30 cm, what is the length of each side?

(A) Each side of the triangle is 15 cm.

(B) Each side of the triangle is 10 cm.

(C) One of the sides is 15 cm, while the other sides are 7 cm and 8 cm, respectively.

(D) One of the sides of the triangle is 10 cm, while the other sides are 12 cm and 8 cm, respectively.

(10) Calculate the area of a triangle 8 cm high and 10 cm wide.

(A) 80 cm

(B) 40 cm

(C) 40 cm^2

(D) 80 cm^2

(11) A triangle is 24 cm from one side to the other and 20 cm from the base to the top. Calculate the area of the triangle.

(A) 480 cm

(B) 240 cm

(C) 480 cm^2

(D) 240 cm^2

(12) Calculate the base of a triangle with a 300 cm^2 area if the height of the triangle is 20 cm.

(A) 20 cm

(B) 30 cm

(C) 45 cm

(D) 60 cm

(13) Find the perimeter of a parallelogram with adjacent sides measuring 10 cm and 12 cm.

(A) 22 cm

(B) 30 cm

(C) 60 cm

(D) 44 cm

(14) What is the sum of the adjacent sides of a parallelogram if the perimeter of the parallelogram is 80 cm?

(A) 10 cm

(B) 20 cm

(C) 40 cm

(D) 60 cm

(15) What is the second side of a parallelogram with an 80 cm perimeter if one of the sides measures 25 cm?

(A) 20 cm

(B) 25 cm

(C) 15 cm

(D) 30 cm

(16) A parallelogram is 15 cm tall and has a base of 20 cm. Find its area.

(A) 150 cm^2

(B) 300 cm^2

(C) 400 cm^2

(D) 250 cm^2

(17) Calculate the height of a parallelogram if the area of the parallelogram is 300 cm^2 and its base is 15 cm.

(A) 20 cm

(B) 30 cm

(C) 45 cm

(D) 15 cm

(18) What is the formula for calculating the area of a circle?

(A) πr^2

(B) $2\pi r^2$

(C) πr

(D) πr^3

(19) Calculate the area of a circle of radius 7 cm. Round to the nearest whole number.

(A) 154 cm

(B) 154 cm^2

(C) 308 cm^2

(D) 77 cm^2

(20) What is the radius of a circle if the area of the circle is 224 cm^2? Give the answer to the nearest whole number.

(A) 22 cm

(B) 8 cm

(C) 21 cm

(D) 25 cm

(21) What is the formula for calculating the circumference of a circle?

(A) $2\pi r$

(B) $3\pi r$

(C) $2\pi r^2$

(D) $2\pi r^3$

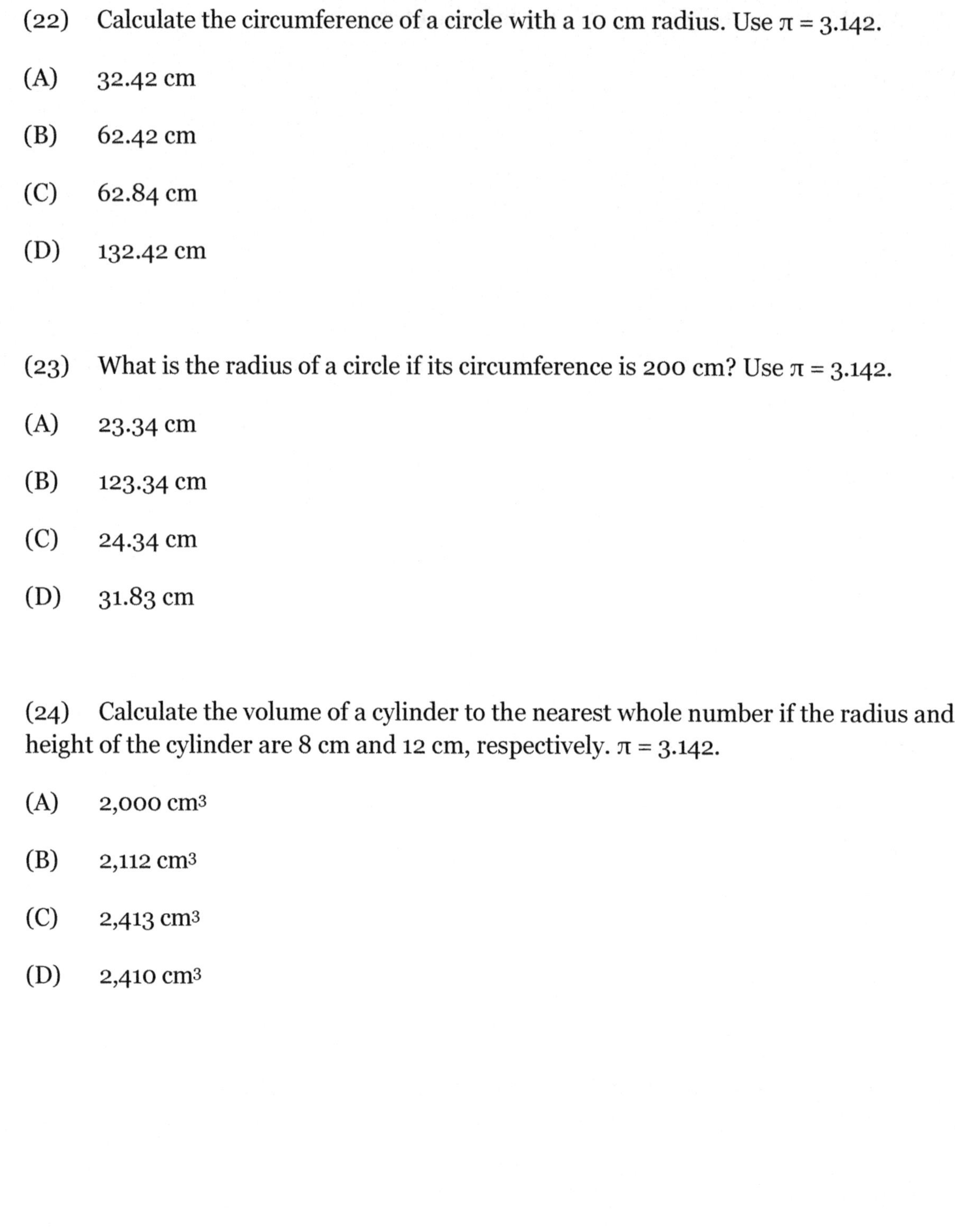

(22) Calculate the circumference of a circle with a 10 cm radius. Use $\pi = 3.142$.

(A) 32.42 cm

(B) 62.42 cm

(C) 62.84 cm

(D) 132.42 cm

(23) What is the radius of a circle if its circumference is 200 cm? Use $\pi = 3.142$.

(A) 23.34 cm

(B) 123.34 cm

(C) 24.34 cm

(D) 31.83 cm

(24) Calculate the volume of a cylinder to the nearest whole number if the radius and height of the cylinder are 8 cm and 12 cm, respectively. $\pi = 3.142$.

(A) 2,000 cm^3

(B) 2,112 cm^3

(C) 2,413 cm^3

(D) 2,410 cm^3

(25) Find the height of a cylinder with a 600 cm^3 volume if the radius of the cylinder is 10 cm. Use $\pi = 3.142$. Express your answer in one decimal place.

(A) 3.8 cm

(B) 2.7 cm

(C) 1.9 cm

(D) 1.5 cm

(26) Find the radius of a cylinder if the volume of the cylinder is 800 cm^3 and it is 12 cm tall. Round your answer to the nearest tenth.

(A) 5.6 cm

(B) 4.7 cm

(C) 4.6 cm

(D) 5.7 cm

(27) What is the total surface area of a cylinder if the cylinder is 20 cm tall and its radius is 5 cm? Round to the nearest whole number.

(A) 943 cm^2

(B) 945 cm^2

(C) 786 cm^2

(D) 853 cm^2

(28) Given that the total surface area of a cylinder is 1,571 cm^2 and the radius of the cylinder is 15 cm, find its height.

(A) 2.3 cm

(B) 3.4 cm

(C) 1.67 cm

(D) 1.76 cm

(29) Which of the following is the formula for calculating the perimeter of a trapezoid?

(A) P = (a + b)/(b + c)

(B) P = a + b + c + d

(C) P = (a + b) * (b + c)

(D) P = (a + b) – (b + c)

(30) What is the perimeter of a trapezoid with sides that measure 6 cm, 8 cm, 10 cm and 12 cm?

(A) 63.63 cm

(B) 8 cm

(C) 36 cm

(D) 45 cm

(31) If three sides of a trapezoid are 10 cm, 11 cm and 12 cm, find the length of the fourth side of the trapezoid if its perimeter is 50 cm.

(A) 18 cm

(B) 15 cm

(C) 17 cm

(D) 19 cm

(32) How long is the fourth side of a trapezoid with a 60 cm perimeter if three sides of the trapezoid are 12 cm, 15 cm and 18 cm?

(A) 20 cm

(B) 15 cm

(C) 23 cm

(D) 18 cm

(33) What is the area of a trapezoid that is 15 cm tall if the bases of the trapezoid are 10 cm and 12 cm?

(A) 180 cm^2

(B) 210 cm^2

(C) 165 cm^2

(D) 175 cm^2

(34) What is the height of a trapezoid with bases that measure 12 cm and 8 cm if the area of the trapezoid is 200 cm^2?

(A) 25 cm

(B) 20 cm

(C) 15 cm

(D) 30 cm

(35) Which of the following is true about a cube?

(A) A cube is a three-dimensional shape with 6 faces, 12 edges and 8 vertices.

(B) A cube is a three-dimensional shape with 8 faces, 12 edges and 6 vertices.

(C) A cube is a three-dimensional shape with 6 faces, 8 edges and 8 vertices.

(D) A cube is a three-dimensional shape with 6 faces, 12 edges and 12 vertices.

(36) Calculate the volume of a cube with 10 cm sides.

(A) 30 cm^3

(B) 30 cm

(C) 100 cm^3

(D) 1,000 cm^3

(37) What is the length of a cube if the volume of the cube is 2,744 cm^3?

(A) 12 cm

(B) 15 cm

(C) 18 cm

(D) 14 cm

(38) Calculate the lateral surface area of a cuboid that has a 12 cm length, 10 cm height and 15 cm width.

(A) 550 cm^2

(B) 540 cm^2

(C) 500 cm^2

(D) 600 cm^2

(39) If the lateral surface area of a cuboid is 1,000 cm^2 and the cuboid is 20 cm tall, find the sum of its width and length.

(A) 20 cm

(B) 30 cm

(C) 25 cm

(D) 50 cm

(40) The perimeter of the base of a cuboid 20 cm tall is 30 cm. Calculate the lateral surface area of the cuboid.

(A) 650 cm^2

(B) 550 cm^2

(C) 450 cm^2

(D) 600 cm^2

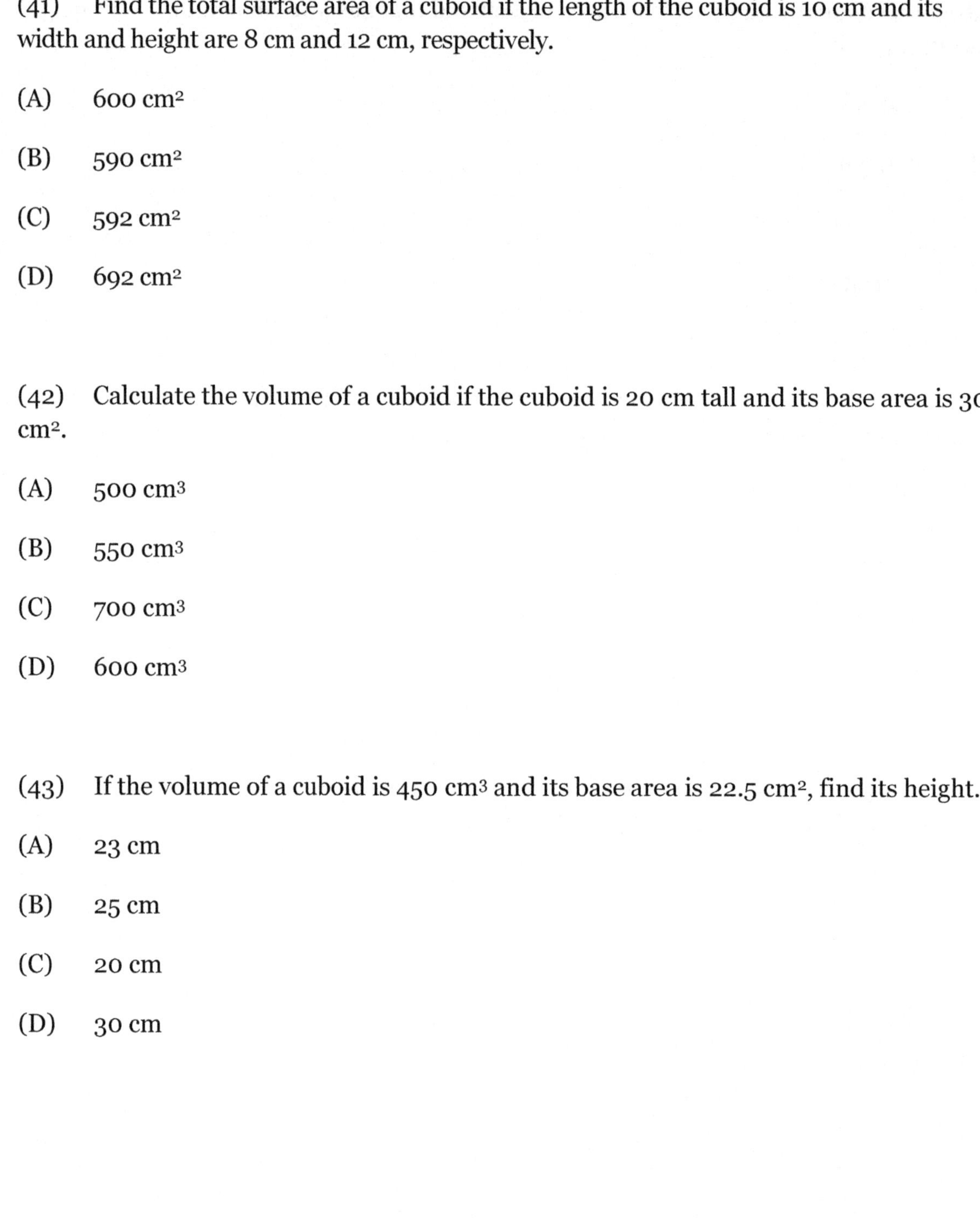

(41) Find the total surface area of a cuboid if the length of the cuboid is 10 cm and its width and height are 8 cm and 12 cm, respectively.

(A) 600 cm^2

(B) 590 cm^2

(C) 592 cm^2

(D) 692 cm^2

(42) Calculate the volume of a cuboid if the cuboid is 20 cm tall and its base area is 30 cm^2.

(A) 500 cm^3

(B) 550 cm^3

(C) 700 cm^3

(D) 600 cm^3

(43) If the volume of a cuboid is 450 cm^3 and its base area is 22.5 cm^2, find its height.

(A) 23 cm

(B) 25 cm

(C) 20 cm

(D) 30 cm

(44) What is the formula for calculating the area of a rhombus with diagonals d1 and d2?

(A) (d1 + d2) * 2

(B) (d1 * d2)/2

(C) (d1 * d2) + 2

(D) (d1 + d2) – 2

(45) Calculate the area of a rhombus if its base is 25 cm and it is 10 cm tall.

(A) 500 cm^2

(B) 250 cm^2

(C) 300 cm^2

(D) 550 cm^2

(46) If the area of a rhombus is 200 cm^2 and one of the diagonals is 10 cm, calculate the second diagonal.

(A) 40 cm

(B) 60 cm

(C) 20 cm

(D) 35 cm

(47) How tall is a rhombus if the base area and area of the rhombus are 25 cm and 120 cm^2, respectively?

(A) 5 cm

(B) 5.2 cm

(C) 4.8 cm

(D) 3.6 cm

(48) What is the sum of the probability that an event will occur and the probability that the event will not occur?

(A) 1

(B) 2

(C) 0

(D) 10

(49) There are three red balls, two yellow balls and five blue balls in a basket. What is the probability of picking a yellow ball from the basket?

(A) 2/15

(B) 2/10

(C) 1/5

(D) 3/15

(50) What is the probability of picking a black ball if there are 5 five black balls and 10 yellow balls in a soccer room?

(A) 2/3

(B) 3/4

(C) 1/3

(D) 4/5

(51) If the probability that an event will not occur is 2/5, what is the probability that it will occur?

(A) 2/5

(B) 3/5

(C) 5/7

(D) 1/4

(52) If Terry rolls a standard six-sided dice, what is the probability that he will roll a 3?

(A) 2/5

(B) 1/6

(C) 3/5

(D) 5/6

(53) What is the mean value of 7, 9 and 14?

(A) 9

(B) 10

(C) 12

(D) 15

(54) Find the value of x if 3 + 10 + 7 + 4 + x = 35.

(A) 10

(B) 12

(C) 15

(D) 11

(55) Find the mean score of the footballers represented in the frequency table below to the nearest whole number.

Player	Number of Goals
Messi	35
Ronaldo	30
Lewandoski	35
Immobile	40
Mbappe	40

(A) 36

(B) 37

(C) 38

(D) 40

(56) Find the mode of 2, 3, 3, 4, 6, 7, 7, 7, 8, 9, 9, 1, 1.

(A) 2

(B) 9

(C) 7

(D) 10

Reading Test 3: Passages

Passage 1: Must-Have Digital Education Tools for Teachers

Teaching can be time-consuming and sometimes overwhelming. With several classes to handle and assignments to attend to, you may miss lunch breaks or have little time to rest after a hectic day at work.

However, you do not have to work around the clock every day. You deserve a rest. With the following important digital education tools, you will enhance your overall performance as a teacher and be able to take a rest when necessary.

Canva

More than ever before, visual aids are becoming integral teaching tools. While some are readily available, you also have to sometimes create personalized visual teaching aids. A good tool for that is Canva.

With Canva, you can create informative infographics, graphs and other educational visuals to improve your teaching and help your students learn better. With a simple learning curve, you can learn how to create intuitive and informative visual aids for all categories of students in no time.

Teaglo

Teaglo is a teachers-only social network platform. Teachers can interact with their colleagues around the world, seek their assistance and exchange ideas. When you create a profile on this platform, you make yourself visible to all of your colleagues who are active on Teaglo.

If you are looking for teaching opportunities abroad, recruiting schools can notice your profile and reach out to you with job offers. Hence, your profile must be attractive enough for potential recruiters. Aside from your educational qualifications, you should include other personal details, such as hobbies, certifications, etc.

Do you have some teaching resources and tips to share with your colleagues? You can do that on Teaglo and rub minds with others too. With input from others who are active on the platform, you can take teaching to the next level.

WeTransfer

Transferring files to your colleagues has never been easier. WeTransfer allows you to easily share large files with your colleagues.

Not only is WeTransfer free, but users are not mandated to create an account before they can use the platform. Whenever you have a file to transfer, simply upload the file, enter the recipient's email address and you are ready to go.

Edmodo

Edmodo is another teaching tool you should try. It is an educational network where teachers and students from different parts of the world can connect and share ideas. On the platform, users can create groups to collaborate with like-minded teachers and create educational materials.

As a teacher, you can use the platform to measure your students' performance. When necessary, you can contact their parents to enable you to create personalized learning experiences.

Teaching will be fun and effective with these tools. With them, you have everything you need to become a more efficient teacher and thus have a positive impact on your students.

Passage 2: Essential Teaching Skills for Modern Teachers

Effective teaching goes beyond being armed with a degree and the ability to read and write. That is just the beginning. Today, you must acquire some skills as a modern teacher to enable you to effectively discharge your teaching responsibilities. The skills below will make you not only a teacher, but a professional and effective one.

Patience

A classroom is made up of a mixture of students from different backgrounds and abilities. Their learning styles and attention spans differ as well. While some of your students may show a positive attitude toward learning and take their homework seriously, others may show a nonchalant attitude. This means that you should understand your students and use patience when dealing with those with learning challenges. With patience, you can guide slow learners until they make the necessary changes or progress.

Critical Thinking

Critical thinking is a must-have skill you need in order to identify the best teaching techniques for your students. This is especially true in view of their diverse intellectual abilities and learning progress. With this skill, you will easily identify the best teaching techniques that will enable you to reach every member of your class.

Thus, with critical thinking, you will be able to strike a balance between your expectations and your students' performance. For instance, while some members of your class may be fast learners and meet your expectations, others will fall behind. Your critical thinking skills will come into play, as they will help you find common ground for teaching all students, irrespective of their varied abilities.

Communication

As a teacher, you can communicate with your students using three communication channels. You can write a message down or speak it. Body language is a third important communication tool. Through gestures and facial expressions, you can convey your message to your students. If your students always struggle to understand you, work on your communication skills.

Leadership

Teachers are leaders. Both inside the classroom and elsewhere, you must display leadership skills for all to see. With your leadership skills, you will not struggle with shaping your students' behavior, especially if you set a good example for them to imitate.

Show your passion for learning and teaching, and let your students take a cue from that. If circumstances permit, you can accept additional responsibilities, such as leading a special club for drama or sports. In no time, some of your students will be inspired to follow you.

Passage 3: Fitness Tips for Healthy Living

Healthy living is everyone's dream. This is because whoever enjoys good health has the capacity to do their job to the best of their abilities, pursue a career, study for a university degree and live their dream. Consider the following fitness tips that can boost your health and allow you to live the life of your dreams.

Stay Hydrated

The human body is made up of approximately 70 percent water. As an adult, you need about eight cups of water daily, according to experts. This amount of water will replace whatever fluids you lose during your daily activities and will help your body function properly. Otherwise, you may suffer from dehydration, a medical condition that will sap you of energy. As a result, you will end up dragging yourself throughout the day.

To get the needed amount of water, eat water-rich fruits or vegetables, such as cucumbers and watermelons. This is to complement your regular water intake before, during, or after a meal. Remember, water is best for hydration. The rule of thumb is not to wait until you are thirsty before you drink water. Drink enough water as you go about your daily activities to ensure that you are hydrated throughout the day.

Exercise Regularly

Working out regularly is another fitness tip you should include in your fitness bucket list. If your job description involves a sedentary lifestyle, you must learn to burn excess fat that your body accumulates while sitting by engaging in simple workouts such as jogging, running, jumping rope and others.

Engaging in these activities will help you burn excess fat and serve as a preventive measure against becoming overweight or obese. Obese and overweight people are prone to medical conditions such as heart disease and diabetes. If you use public transportation, get off a few stops away from your office and walk the remaining distance. Repeat the same when returning home in the evening. If you are a vehicle owner, park your vehicle some blocks from your office. Learn to use the stairs instead of the elevator except when absolutely necessary.

Eat Fruits and Veggies

Fruits and vegetables are not only delicious, but they also contribute significantly to good health. They are rich in vitamins. Some commonly available fruits are rich in fiber, too, and will help you reach your weight-loss goal. That is in addition to their vitamin C content, which boosts your immunity. Cucumbers, watermelons, apples, spinach and carrots are some veggies and fruits you should always include in your meals.

You can stay physically fit if you watch your diet, always stay hydrated and regularly engage in enjoyable exercise. This will boost your immunity and help you ward off diseases that may stand between you and good health.

Reading Test 3: Questions

(1) What example does the passage give of how teaching can be overwhelming?

(A) A teacher's workload

(B) Poor pay

(C) Missing lunch breaks

(D) All of the above

(2) What are visual aids?

(A) Teaching materials designed to make teaching more effective

(B) Teaching materials for young students

(C) Teaching materials for beginner teachers

(D) Necessary tools for all teachers

(3) Which of the following is not a visual aid?

(A) Graphs

(B) Infographics

(C) A table of contents

(D) None of the above

(4) What does a *simple learning curve* indicate?

(A) Students can learn how to use the tool easily.

(B) Teachers can learn how to use the tool easily.

(C) It's best not to use a particular tool.

(D) You can learn how to use the tool at your convenience.

(5) Which of the following is a teachers-only social network platform?

(A) Canva

(B) Teaglo

(C) WeTransfer

(D) Teachers Connect

(6) What is WeTransfer designed for?

(A) Connecting teachers

(B) Transferring teachers from one school to another

(C) Transferring files

(D) Sharing social media tips

(7) What do you stand to gain from sharing resources with your colleagues?

(A) It makes you popular among your colleagues.

(B) It puts you in line for a promotion.

(C) It is your contribution to growing the teaching profession.

(D) It enhances your file-sharing skills.

(8) Which of the following allows teachers and students to connect?

(A) Edmodo

(B) WeConnect

(C) WeTransfer

(D) TeachersConnect

(9) What important information do you need to transfer files on WeTransfer?

(A) Recipient's location and email address

(B) Recipient's phone number and email address

(C) Recipient's email address

(D) Recipient's physical location

(10) Sharing useful tips and resources is easier on which platform?

(A) WeTransfer

(B) WeConnect

(C) Teaglo

(D) Edmodo

(11) How can users collaborate on Edmodo?

(A) By forming caucuses

(B) By creating goal-oriented groups

(C) By associating according to years of experience

(D) By forming associations by location

(12) How can teachers use Edmodo to assist their students?

(A) By using it to grade their scores

(B) By using it to create personalized teaching for them

(C) By using it to introduce them to social networking

(D) By using it to teach them valuable life hacks

(13) If you are looking for teaching opportunities, which of the platforms should you focus on?

(A) Teaglo

(B) Edmodo

(C) WeConnect

(D) TeachersConnect

(14) What does *not mandated* mean as used in the passage?

(A) Recommended

(B) Not compulsory

(C) Habitual

(D) Conditional

(15) To attract more recruiters on Teaglo, which of the following should you include in your profile?

(A) Location and age

(B) Hobbies and certifications

(C) Age and years of experience

(D) Hobbies and preferences

(16) What does *rub minds with* mean in the passage?

(A) Exchange personal contacts

(B) Exchange ideas

(C) Become physically attracted to each other

(D) Befriend others

(17) Which of the following is a synonym for *intuitive*?

(A) Facts-based

(B) Feelings-based

(C) Influenced by the environment

(D) None of the above

(18) *Hectic,* as used in the passage, means what?

(A) Cumbersome

(B) Stressful

(C) Busy

(D) Suffocating

(19) What does *input* mean as used in the passage?

(A) Contributions

(B) Assessment

(C) Personal conviction

(D) Supervision

(20) Which of the following can contextually replace *armed with*?

(A) Weaponized

(B) Equipped with

(C) Paid for

(D) None of the above

(21) What type of context clue is demonstrated by this expression: "...take their homework seriously, others may show a nonchalant attitude toward learning"?

(A) Synonym context clue

(B) Antonym context clue

(C) General context clue

(D) Conditional context clue

(22) What factors should you consider when dealing with students?

(A) Their learning styles and attention spans

(B) Their nonchalant attitudes towards learning

(C) Their natural dispositions

(D) All of the above

(23) Why is patience crucial to teaching?

(A) It shows attention to detail.

(B) It shows consideration for students' individual differences.

(C) None of the above.

(D) A and B.

(24) Define *critical thinking* according to the passage.

(A) The ability to accurately criticize a line of thought

(B) The ability to discern the best teaching technique

(C) The ability to differentiate between good and bad

(D) A self-taught skill for self-sufficiency

(25) How important is critical thinking to effective teaching?

(A) It makes you an effective teacher.

(B) There is no connection between the two.

(C) It helps you grade faster.

(D) Critical thinking has little effect on teaching.

(26) What are the three communication styles?

(A) Verbal, written and body language

(B) Verbal, body language and facial expression

(C) Gestures, body language and written

(D) Written, body language and verbal

(27) Facial expression is an example of which communication style?

(A) Verbal

(B) Written

(C) Body language

(D) None of the above

(28) Which of these skills should you work on if your students always have difficulty understanding you?

(A) Critical thinking

(B) Communication

(C) Leadership

(D) Personal behavior

(29) What is another word or expression for *exemplary*?

(A) Worthy of imitation

(B) Confusing

(C) Used as examples

(D) Worthy of celebration

(30) What does *take a cue from* mean?

(A) Celebrate

(B) Duplicate

(C) Imitate

(D) Inculcate

(31) What impact can showing leadership traits have on students?

(A) It helps them aspire to leadership positions in the future.

(B) It helps shape them into well-behaved students.

(C) It can help them become political leaders.

(D) All of the above.

(32) What does *to reach every member of your class* mean?

(A) To call on every single student

(B) To take them out for a picnic

(C) To ensure that everyone understands you

(D) To put them in different classes

(33) How can teaching test your patience?

(A) It will test your ability to deal with your students according to their attention spans.

(B) It will test your ability to shout at your students.

(C) It will test your ability to teach them together.

(D) It cannot test your patience.

(34) What does *goes beyond* mean?

(A) More than a certificate and ability to read and write is required to become an effective teacher.

(B) You are not qualified to teach with just a teaching certificate and the ability to read and write.

(C) You need special training aside from your teaching certificate.

(D) You need special certificates in addition to your ability to read and write.

(35) A lack of patience while teaching may result in what?

(A) Loss of interest in teaching

(B) Loss of appetite

(C) Hatred for the students

(D) Nonchalant attitude toward teaching

(36) Which of the following is a synonym of *disposition*?

(A) Temperament

(B) Skills

(C) Natural feelings

(D) Lack of enthusiasm

(37) Which of the following skills will help you adopt the best teaching technique?

(A) Communication

(B) Leadership

(C) Critical thinking

(D) Patience

(38) Which of the following is correct?

(A) About half of the human body is composed of water.

(B) Almost three-quarters of the human body is composed of water.

(C) One-third of the human body is composed of water.

(D) Three-fifths of the human body is composed of water.

(39) What amount of water do you need daily as an adult?

(A) 5 cups

(B) 8 cups

(C) 10 cups

(D) 2 cups

(40) What can result from a water shortage in the body?

(A) Hives

(B) Cancer

(C) Dehydration

(D) Infection

(41) What impact can insufficient water have on your body?

(A) It will sap you of energy.

(B) It will renew your energy.

(C) It will make you smart.

(D) It has no significant effect on your body.

(42) What should be the primary source of hydration for the body?

(A) Soft drinks

(B) Processed fruit drinks

(C) Water

(D) All of the above

(43) When is the best time to drink water?

(A) When you are thirsty

(B) Before you are thirsty

(C) At bedtime

(D) When you wake up in the morning

(44) Which of the following fruits can support hydration?

(A) Carrots and papayas

(B) Watermelons

(C) Apples and grapes

(D) All types of berries

(45) What does *sedentary lifestyle* mean?

(A) Working too much

(B) Standing for too long

(C) Sitting for too long at a time

(D) Drinking too much water

(46) What simple exercise can boost your fitness level?

(A) Marathon running

(B) Weight lifting

(C) Jogging

(D) Skiing

(47) Why are workouts good for fitness?

(A) They help you stay hydrated.

(B) They keep you full and reduce your food consumption.

(C) They burn excess body fat and keep you healthy.

(D) All of the above.

(48) What medical conditions are obese and overweight people prone to?

(A) Cholera and typhoid

(B) Acute fever and rheumatism

(C) Diabetes and heart disease

(D) Malnutrition and syphilis

(49) If you use public transportation, how can you work on your fitness?

(A) By standing on the bus when commuting to work

(B) By making sure you walk some distance daily

(C) By drinking tea while in transit

(D) By dancing while walking

(50) Why are fruits and vegetables good for fitness?

(A) They are rich in vitamins.

(B) They are rich in vitamin C and potassium.

(C) They are rich in vitamin D and cholesterol.

(D) None of the above

(51) What role does vitamin C play in fitness?

(A) It boosts the body's immune system.

(B) It regulates the body's water content.

(C) It nourishes the body.

(D) It replaces worn-out tissues.

(52) What role does fiber play in fitness?

(A) It supports weight loss.

(B) It supports cholesterol accumulation.

(C) It supports the body's immune system.

(D) It fights fatigue.

(53) How can vehicle owners include walking in their daily activities?

(A) By walking on weekends

(B) By walking on public holidays

(C) By creating walking opportunities for themselves throughout the day

(D) All of the above

(54) According to the passage, what is the danger of using the elevator?

(A) Risk of laziness

(B) Risk of power failure

(C) Lower levels of physical fitness

(D) None of the above

(55) What does *bucket list* mean?

(A) A list of items you put in a basket as a reminder

(B) A list of buckets you wish to buy

(C) A list of things you want to do

(D) A list of general things and items

(56) What can you deduce from the passage?

(A) Physical activity promotes physical fitness.

(B) Physical activity can promote weight gain.

(C) Eating fruits and vegetables alone is good for your health.

(D) A sedentary lifestyle is recommended for young people.

Writing Test 3: Questions

(1) Identify the odd member of the lists below.

(A) Indefinite and possessive adjectives

(B) Possessive and demonstrative adjectives

(C) Interrogative and descriptive adjectives

(D) Number and indefinite adjectives

(2) What is the function of interrogative adjectives?

(A) Interrogation

(B) Itemizing

(C) Scientific reasoning

(D) Collecting information from patients in hospitals

(3) What are indefinite adjectives used for?

(A) To describe living and nonliving things

(B) To describe emotions

(C) To describe nonspecific nouns

(D) To describe nonspecific nouns and specific pronouns

(4) Which of the following adjectives answers the question, "How many boys are in the vehicle?"

(A) Interrogative adjectives

(B) Questionnaire adjectives

(C) Number adjectives

(D) Possessive adjectives

(5) Identify the sentence that contains an interrogative adjective.

(A) What is he doing there?

(B) Will she come over today?

(C) Can I go now?

(D) Since when did he leave home?

(6) What are adverbial conjunctions used for?

(A) To join relative clauses to one another

(B) To join subordinate clauses to one another

(C) To join independent clauses to one another

(D) To join different types of clauses to one another

(7) What does a number adjective do?

(A) It helps describe the number of elements in a group.

(B) It helps find more information about the quantity of an object.

(C) It helps describe the collective number of the features of elements in a group.

(D) It helps describe the number of elements in a group in relation to the elements.

(8) What is a common error many people make when using adverbs?

(A) They place an adverb before a verb in a sentence.

(B) They never use adverbs in a sentence.

(C) They place an adverb after a verb in a sentence.

(D) They do not know the appropriate number of adverbs to be used in a sentence.

(9) Which of the sentences below is incorrect?

(A) He left home because he was late hurriedly.

(B) She dances beautifully.

(C) He fixed the problem perfectly.

(D) The boys carefully placed the eggs in the egg trays.

(10) What is the common error with *enough* usage?

(A) It is commonly used after the adjective or adverb it should modify.

(B) It is commonly used before the adjective or adverb it should modify.

(C) It is commonly used between the adjective or adverb it should modify.

(D) It is commonly used in place of the adjective or adverb it should modify.

(11) Identify the error in this sentence: "The girl and her twin sister are great dancer."

(A) Pronoun-noun agreement error

(B) Adverb-adverb agreement error

(C) Noun-noun agreement error

(D) Independent clauses agreement error

(12) How do coordinating conjunction errors occur?

(A) When two independent clauses are joined with a coordinating conjunction without a comma before the conjunction

(B) When two independent clauses are joined with a coordinating conjunction before the appropriate adverb

(C) When two dependent clauses are joined with a coordinating conjunction before the appropriate adverb

(D) When two independent clauses are joined with a coordinating conjunction without a comma after the conjunction

(13) If a writer mistakenly uses *or* for *neither* or *nor* for *either*, what type of error has the writer made?

(A) A coordinating conjunction error

(B) A subordinating conjunction error

(C) A correlative conjunction error

(D) A parallel structure error

(14) Which of the following sentences is incorrect?

(A) Her boss complemented her for a job well done.

(B) She sent a complimentary card to her colleague.

(C) Everything is moving on as planned.

(D) The boys will soon be done with their assignments.

(15) Identify the error-free sentence from the list below.

(A) She speaks English with an African assent.

(B) Sci-fi movies create impressive allusion.

(C) Everyone is concerned about the potential affect of the unfortunate incident.

(D) The principal was unavoidably absent from the seminar.

(16) Identify the error in this sentence: "Olu love going to the gym."

(A) Noun-pronoun error

(B) Subject-verb agreement error

(C) Pronoun-antecedent error

(D) Adjectival error

(17) What is a dangling modifier?

(A) A phrase or clause that is not clearly or logically connected to the words it modifies

(B) A conjunction that is used too many times

(C) An adjective that modifies an adverb

(D) An adverb that modifies a noun

(18) Identify the redundancy in this sentence: “While reversing back, the driver hit a pole.”

(A) While

(B) While reversing

(C) Reversing

(D) Back

(19) What is wrong with this sentence: “He sings, dances and he can write lyrics”?

(A) It has a parallel connection error.

(B) It has a dangling modifier.

(C) It has a parallel structure error.

(D) It is error-free.

(20) Rewrite this sentence: “Hitting your goals in life may be quite difficult, challenging and may be taxing too.”

(A) Hitting your goals in life may be quite challenging, difficult and maybe taxing as well.

(B) Hitting your goals in life may be quite challenging, difficult and may be taxing too.

(C) Hitting your goals in life may be quite difficult, challenging and taxing too.

(D) Hitting your goals in life may be quite taxing, challenging and may be difficult too.

(21) How can you avoid parallel structure errors while writing?

(A) By using the appropriate adjectives

(B) By ensuring that the phrases or words you use in a series are of the same form

(C) By ensuring that the phrases or words you use in a series are of similar meaning and intonation

(D) By ensuring that the phrases or words you use in a series are different in meaning

(22) Which of the following sentence(s) is correct?

(A) He loves her but still yet, he hasn't proposed to her.

(B) He loves her, but he still hasn't proposed to her.

(C) He loves her, but he hasn't proposed to her.

(D) B and C.

(23) Which of the following is a list of redundant words and phrases?

(A) Forever and ever, close proximity and absolutely certain

(B) Past experience, isolated words and plus in addition

(C) Compete with each other, postpone until later and in addition to

(D) Added bonus, revert back and absolutely important

(24) Which of the following sentences is wrong?

(A) Tolu and Kike are lovely friends.

(B) She dance like a pop star.

(C) Nobody saw it coming.

(D) Everybody loves good food.

(25) How can you prevent redundancy while writing?

(A) By using phrasal verbs

(B) By using idiomatic expressions

(C) By becoming familiar with such expressions and avoiding them while writing

(D) By using such expressions sparingly while writing

(26) The error that occurs when there is no agreement between a pronoun and its antecedent is known as what?

(A) Antecedent-pronoun error

(B) Pronoun-antecedent agreement error

(C) Pronoun-antecedent connection error

(D) Antecedent-pronoun connection error

(27) What is the most effective preventive measure against pronoun-antecedent errors?

(A) Be familiar with nouns and pronouns

(B) Identify the appropriate pronouns for each noun and use them accordingly

(C) Learn many pronoun usage examples

(D) Avoid using pronouns while writing

(28) "The couple has a beautiful house." Identify the error in the sentence.

(A) Subject-verb agreement error

(B) Pronoun-antecedent error

(C) No error

(D) Sentence structure error

(29) Using the wrong verb for a subject results in what type of error?

(A) Subject agreement error

(B) Verb agreement error

(C) Verb-subject agreement error

(D) Subject-verb agreement error

(30) Which of the following pairs of subjects and verbs is not correct?

(A) Ben and his friends/dance.

(B) Kenny and his twin sister/want.

(C) The cat and its kittens/loves.

(D) None of the above.

(31) How can you differentiate between a singular and a plural noun?

(A) A singular noun does not usually end with an *s*, while a plural noun does.

(B) A plural noun does not end with an *s*, while a singular noun does.

(C) A singular pronoun does not end with *-ied* when pluralized, while a plural noun does.

(D) Plural nouns are used for simple sentences, while singular nouns are used for complex sentences.

(32) What is the similarity between a singular noun and a plural verb?

(A) Both usually end with an *s*.

(B) Both usually do not end with an *s*.

(C) Both are used primarily in compound-complex sentences.

(D) Both are used in unique writing circumstances.

(33) Which of the following is not a collection of singular verbs in third person?

(A) Does, goes, walks and sing

(B) Sings, plays, sings and dances

(C) Writes, sleeps and plays

(D) None of the above

(34) When should the letter *i* be capitalized?

(A) When it appears at the beginning of a sentence, begins a proper name or is used as the first-person pronoun

(B) At the start of a word

(C) When any of its contraction forms is used in a sentence

(D) None of the above

(35) Which of the following is correct?

(A) When will the program begin, Senator?

(B) I will visit the halloween next week.

(C) i've been informed of the meeting in advance.

(D) All of the above.

(36) What is an exclamation mark used for?

(A) To show the connection between words

(B) To express strong emotions

(C) For interrogation

(D) To indicate the end of a sentence

(37) What are the two functions of an apostrophe?

(A) To indicate possession and ownership

(B) To indicate ownership and contraction

(C) To indicate ownership and relationship between two objects

(D) To separate the items in a list and show the relationship between two objects

(38) In which of the following sentences is the apostrophe misused?

(A) Olu and his brother's friends are here.

(B) My mother's colleagues will pay us a visit tomorrow.

(C) I will visit my sisters' at work next week.

(D) None of the above.

(39) "I love the book *The secret of business success*." What is the error in the book's title?

(A) Spelling error

(B) Typo

(C) Capitalization error

(D) Punctuation error

(40) Rewrite: "I will be available for the next tour of the eiffel tower."

(A) I will be available for the next tour of the Eiffel Tower.

(B) I will be available for the next tour of the Eiffel tower.

(C) I will be available for the next tour of the eiffel Tower.

(D) I will be available for the next Tour of the eiffel tower.

Essay 5: Is Gun Control the Solution to Crime?

In the United States, an average of 13 children under the age of 19 die by gunfire each day. Higher numbers are injured daily, making homicide the number two cause of death of children between the ages of 10 and 19. It is the leading cause of death among Black males in the country. This raises the question, is gun control the needed solution for increasing crime rates in the United States?

Citing the case of a mass murderer who killed 22 people in El Paso, Texas, in August 2019, the *Crimson White* launched a campaign in favor of gun control in the United States. According to the media house's staff columnist, Heather Gann, the country would have been spared such killings if the government had put a stricter gun control policy in place.

An example of the connection between gun control and reduction in crime rates is the case of Michael Ryan, who was responsible for a massacre in the United Kingdom in 1987. After he murdered 16 people with his registered weapon before committing suicide, the government regulated the use of semiautomatic weapons in the country. The result has been tremendous.

Since 1996, the country has witnessed just one mass shooting, while the United States recorded 255 mass shootings within the first eight months in 2019. Gun control proponents attribute the skyrocketing rates of mass shootings in the United States to easy access to guns in the country. They believe that introducing stricter gun control would result in reduced killing and crime rates across the country.

Murder is not the only reason gun control should be of paramount importance to the US government. It's estimated that the country witnessed over 73,500 nonfatal firearm injuries and over 33,600 deaths arising from firearm injuries in 2013 alone. The same year, over 21,000 suicides were recorded in the United States, according to multiple sources. Between 1968 and 2011, over 1.4 million Americans died by firearm.

The National Crime Victimization Survey reported that over 467,000 people were victims of firearm-related crimes in 2011. These mind-blowing reports show a disturbing trend: a lenient firearm policy in the United States has increasingly promoted crime in the country. If the trend continues unabated, the country may witness increasing firearm-related crimes in the future.

However, not everyone is comfortable with gun control in the United States. For instance, the National Rifle Association, a US-based gun rights advocacy group, has consistently fought against gun regulation in the country. The group is of the opinion that gun regulation is not the solution to crime rates in the country and does not support any move by the government to introduce policies that will make guns less accessible to citizens.

Regardless of the NRA's opinion, the government will achieve a good measure of success in its fight against increasing crime rates if it can control gun usage in the country.

Essay 5 Questions

(1) What is the leading cause of death among Black males in the United States?

(A) Drug abuse

(B) Terrorism

(C) Homicide

(D) None of the above

(2) What can you deduce from the passage?

(A) Black Americans are using guns more than their White counterparts.

(B) White Americans are using guns more than their Black counterparts.

(C) Gun possession encourages crime.

(D) The government cannot win the fight against crime.

Essay 6: How Useful Are Social Media Platforms?

The introduction of social media platforms, such as Twitter, Facebook, Instagram and others, has changed the way people connect and communicate. These platforms have made communication a lot easier and faster. Nevertheless, it has not been all fun with these communication tools. They have many disadvantages too.

Over the years, people from different backgrounds have found some flaws in social media. They cite the instances of several criminal cases, such as murders and scams that are perpetrated via these platforms, as their argument against social media's usefulness. Are social media platforms truly dangerous? Let's take a look at them.

Since the introduction of social media, it has been used extensively as a source both for personal and academic research. Using the various platforms, people can utilize educational resources that were previously inaccessible from any part of the world.

LinkedIn, one of the biggest professional social media platforms, has provided over 60 million professionals with a meeting platform where they can market their skills. Millions of people are living their dream lives, thanks to LinkedIn. If you are a professional and crave more exposure, LinkedIn should top your list of social media platforms, where you can get hired by organizations in need of your services. Other platforms have their specific uses too.

Companies are also benefiting from LinkedIn, as it helps them find qualified job seekers and personnel to staff their companies. With the demand for remote jobs and workers increasing astronomically in recent years, social media platforms have become the go-to for employees looking for remote job opportunities and employers looking for competent and qualified employees who can work from any part of the world. This would not have been possible without social media platforms.

According to the *Military Times*, social media has played a significant role in suicide prevention among military personnel in recent years. According to the newspaper, an attempted suicide by a military man was prevented when he used a Facebook post to hint about his intentions. A swift response to the post helped the military avert a suicide attempt.

Since then, the US military has developed various social media sites for veterans to help them with issues, including post-traumatic stress disorder, thus preventing suicide among retired military personnel.

Social media has also helped many people achieve their personal or career goals through the crowdsourcing opportunity it offers. It has empowered thousands of users to change negative attitudes about life and embrace positive change as encouraged through social media posts, comments, videos and motivational talks.

Thus, it can be argued that social media platforms are not all about social networking. They offer job opportunities, provide learning resources and platforms, promote social justice and help people live their dream lives.

Essay 6 Questions

(1) Kenny is a brilliant engineer. Which of the following social media platforms should he concentrate on to meet prospective employers/clients?

(A) Instagram

(B) Facebook

(C) Twitter

(D) LinkedIn

(2) Which of the following is not an advantage of social media?

(A) Job opportunities

(B) Changes in orientation and beliefs

(C) None of the above

(D) A and B

Mathematics Test 3: Answers & Explanations

(1) (B) By the closure of a shape's curves, points and lines.

Geometric shapes are circles, squares, rectangles and triangles, among others, that are formed by the closure of the shape's points, curves and lines.

(2) (C) Two-dimensional and three-dimensional.

Geometric shapes are divided into two-dimensional and three-dimensional shapes. Two-dimensional shapes can be measured using length and width, while three-dimensional shapes can be measured using length, width and height.

(3) (D) 28 cm.

The perimeter of a square where the side is denoted with "a" is 4a.

Thus, the perimeter of the square with sides 7 cm would be 4 * 7 cm = 28 cm.

(4) (C) 15 cm.

Perimeter of the square = 60 cm.

Perimeter of a square of side l =4 l

Hence, 4 l = 60 cm.

To find the side of the square, divide through by 4.

4l/4 = 60 cm/4

l = 15.0 cm.

(5) (D) 100 cm^2.

For a square of side l, the area of the square is $A = l^2$.

Thus, the area of a square with sides 10 cm = $(10\ cm)^2$ = 100 cm^2.

(6) (C) 15 cm.

Area of a square of length l = l^2

Area of the square = 225 cm^2

l^2 = 225 cm^2

Find the square root of both sides.

$\sqrt{l^2} = \sqrt{225\ cm^2}$

l = 15 cm.

(7) (C) 26 cm.

Perimeter of a triangle = a + b + c, where a, b and c are 6 cm, 8 cm and 12 cm, respectively.

Therefore, P = 6 cm + 8 cm + 12 cm = 26 cm.

(8) (B) 18 cm.

Perimeter of a triangle = a + b + c, where a, b and c are 3 cm, 7cm and 8 cm, respectively.

Therefore, P = 3 cm + 7 cm + 8 cm = 18 cm.

(9) (B) Each side of the triangle is 10 cm.

The three sides of an equilateral triangle are equal.

Thus, for a triangle of side lcm, the perimeter is 3l cm.

3l = 30 cm

Divide through by 3.

l = 10 cm.

(10) (C) 40 cm^2.

Height of the triangle, h = 10 cm

Width of the triangle, b = 8 cm

Area = 1/2 * b · h = 1/2 * 8cm * 10 cm

Area = 1/2 * 80 cm = 40 cm^2.

(11) (D) 240 cm^2.

Height of the triangle, h = 20 cm

Width of the triangle, b = 24 cm

Area = 1/2 * b * h = ½ * 20 cm * 24 cm

Area = 1/2 * 480 cm = 240 cm^2.

(12) (B) 30 cm.

Area of a triangle = 1/2 * b * h, where b and h are the base and height of the triangle.

300 cm^2 = 1/2 * b * 20

300 cm^2 = 10b

Divide through by 10.

300 cm^2 = 10b

300 cm^2/10 = 10b/10

30 cm = b.

(13) (D) 44 cm.

Perimeter of a parallelogram is P = 2 (sum of its adjacent sides).

Adjacent sides are 10 cm and 12 cm, respectively.

Sum of the adjacent sides = 10 cm + 12 m = 22 cm

Perimeter = 2 (sum of adjacent sides)

Perimeter = 2 (22 cm) = 44 cm.

(14) (C) 40 cm.

Perimeter of a parallelogram = 2 * sum of adjacent sides

80 cm = 2 (sum of adjacent sides)

Divide through by 2.

80 cm/2 = 2 (sum of adjacent sides)

40 cm = sum of adjacent sides.

(15) (C) 15 cm.

Perimeter of a parallelogram = 2 * sum of adjacent sides

80 cm = 2 (sum of adjacent sides)

Divide through by 2.

80 cm/2 = 2 (sum of adjacent sides)

40 cm = sum of adjacent sides

If the sum of the adjacent sides is 40cm and one of the sides is 25 cm, the second side is 40 cm – 25 cm = 15 cm.

(16) (B) 300 cm^2.

Base of parallelogram = 20 cm

Height of parallelogram = 15 cm

Area of parallelogram = base * height

Area of parallelogram = 20 cm * 15 cm = 300 cm^2.

(17) (A) 20 cm.

Base of parallelogram = 15 cm

Height of parallelogram = x

Area of parallelogram = base * height

300 cm^2 = 15 cm * x

= 300 cm^2 = 15 cmx

Divide through by 15 cm.

20 cm = x.

(18) (A) πr^2.

The area of a radius can be calculated by using the formula $A = \pi r^2$. For a circle of diameter d, the radius is r = d/2. π = 22/7 or 3.142.

(19) (B) 154 cm^2.

Area of circle = πr^2

r = 7 cm

Area of the circle = (22/7) * 7 cm * 7 cm

Area of the circle = 22 * 7 cm = 154 cm^2.

(20) (B) 8 cm.

Area of circle = πr^2

Given: area = 224 cm^2

224 cm^2 = 22/7 * r^2

Multiply by 7 to get rid of the denominator of 22.

7 * 224 cm^2 = 7 * (22/7) * r^2

1568 cm^2 = $22r^2$

Divide through by 22.

1568 cm^2/22 = $22r^2$/22

71.27 cm^2 = r^2

Find the square root of both sides.

$\sqrt{}$71.27 cm^2 = $\sqrt{}r^2$

8.44 cm = r

Thus, r = 8.44 cm.

(21) (A) $2\pi r$.

The distance around a circle is its circumference. The circumference of a circle is calculated with $2\pi r$, where r is the radius of the circle and π is 22/7, or 3.142.

(22) (C) 62.84 cm.

Circumference of the circle = $2\pi r$

r = 10 cm, π = 3.142

Circumference of the circle = 2 * 3.142 * 10 cm = 62.84 cm.

(23) (D) 31.83 cm.

Circumference of the circle = $2\pi r$

Circumference = 200 cm, π = 3.142

200 cm = 2 * 3.142 * r

200 cm = 6.284r

Divide through by 6.284.

200 cm/6.284 = 6.284r/6.284

31.826 cm = r.

(24) (C) 2,413 cm^3.

Radius of the cylinder = 8 cm

Height of the cylinder = 12 cm

Volume of the cylinder = $\pi r^2 h$

Volume of the cylinder = 3.142 * 8 cm * 8 cm * 12 cm

Volume of the cylinder = 2,413.056 cm^3, or 2,413 cm^3 to the nearest whole number.

(25) (C) 1.9 cm.

Radius of the cylinder = 10 cm

Volume of the cylinder = 600 cm^3

Height of the cylinder = x

Volume of a cylinder = $\pi r^2 h$

600 cm^3 = 3.142 * 10 cm * 10 cm * h

600 cm^3 = 314.2 cm^2h

Divide through by $314.2\ cm^2$.

$600\ cm^3/314.2\ cm^2 = 314.2\ cm^2h/314.2\ cm^2$

1.9096 cm =h or h = 1.9 cm to one decimal place.

(26) (C) 4.6 cm.

Volume of the cylinder = $800\ cm^3$

Height of the cylinder = 12 cm

Volume of a cylinder = πr^2h

$800\ cm^3 = 3.142 * 12\ cm * r^2$

$800\ cm^3 = 37.704\ r^2$

Divide both sides by 37.704.

$800\ cm^3/37.704 = 37.704\ r^2/37.704$

$21.22\ cm = r^2$

Find the square root of both sides.

$\sqrt{}21.22\ cm = \sqrt{}r^2$

4.6065 = r, or r = 4.6cm to one decimal place.

(27) (C) $786\ cm^2$.

Radius of the cylinder, r = 5 cm

Height of the cylinder, 20 = 10 cm

Total surface area of the cylinder = $2\pi r\ (r + h)$

TSA = 2 * 3.142 * 5 (5 cm + 20 cm)

TSA = 31.42 (25)

TSA = 785.5 cm^2, or approximately 786 cm^2.

(28) (C) 1.67 cm.

Total surface area of the cylinder = 1,571 cm^2

Total surface area of a cylinder = $2\pi r (r + h)$

1,571 cm^2 = 2 * 3.142 * 15 cm (h + 15 cm)

1,571 cm^2 = 94.26 cm (h + 15 cm)

Divide through by 94.26 cm.

16.67 cm = h + 15 cm

h = 1.67 cm.

(29) (B) P = a + b + c + d

Add all the sides of a trapezoid together to calculate its perimeter. Thus, for a trapezoid of sides a, b, c and d, the perimeter is P = a + b + c + d.

(30) (C) 36 cm.

Perimeter = sum of all sides

Length of sides = 6 cm, 8 cm, 10 cm and 12 cm

Perimeter of the trapezoid = 6 cm + 8 cm + 10 cm + 12 cm = 36 cm.

(31) (C) 17 cm.

Sides of the trapezoid = 10 cm, 11 cm and 12 cm

Fourth side of the trapezoid = x

Perimeter of a trapezoid = sum of all its sides

Thus, 50 cm = 10 cm + 11 cm + 12 cm +x

50 cm = 31 cm + x

50 cm – 33 cm = x

17 cm = x.

(32) (B) 15 cm.

Sides of the trapezoid = 12 cm, 15 cm and 18 cm

Fourth side of the trapezoid = x

Perimeter of a trapezoid = sum of all its sides

Thus, 60 cm = 12 cm + 15 cm + 18 cm +x

60 cm = 45 cm + x

60 cm – 45 cm = x

15 cm = x.

(33) (C) 165 cm^2.

Base a = 10 cm

Base b = 12 cm

Height h = 15 cm

Area A = h (a + b)/2, where h, a and b are the height and the two bases, respectively.

Area of the trapezoid = 15 cm/2 (10 cm + 12 cm)

Area = 7.5 cm (22 cm) = 165 cm^2.

(34) (B) 20 cm.

Base a = 8 cm

Base b = 12 cm

Height h = x

Area = 200 cm^2

Area of a trapezoid = h/2 (a + b)

200 cm^2 = h/2 (8cm + 12 cm)

200 cm^2 = h/2 (20 cm)

200 cm^2 = 10 cmh

Divide through by 10 cm.

200 cm^2/10 cm = 10h/10 cm

20 cm = h.

(35) (A) A cube is a three-dimensional shape with 6 faces, 12 edges and 8 vertices.

A cube is a three-dimensional object with 6 faces, 12 edges and 8 vertices. The only difference between a cube and a cuboid is that a cube has equal length, width and height.

(36) (D) 1,000 cm^3.

Volume of a cube of side l = l^3

Given: length l = 10 cm

Length of the cube = 10 cm

Volume of the cube = 10^3 = 1,000 cm^3.

(37) (D) 14 cm.

Volume of a cube = l^3 where l is the length

Length of the cube = l

Volume of a cube = l^3

2,744 $cm^3 = l^3$

Find the cube root of both sides.

$\sqrt[3]{2,744\ cm^3} = \sqrt[3]{l^3}$

14 cm = l.

(38) (B) 540 cm^2.

Length of the cuboid = 12 cm

Width of the cuboid = 15 cm

Height of the cuboid = 10 cm

Lateral surface area of a cuboid, LSA = 2 (l + b) * h

LSA = 2 (12 cm + 15 cm) * 10 cm

LSA = 20 (27 cm) = 540 cm^2.

(39) (C) 25 cm.

Height = 20 cm

Sum of its length and width = l + b

LSA = 2 (l + b) * h

1,000 cm^2 = 2 * 20 cm (l + b)

1,000 cm^2 = 40 cm (l + b)

1,000 cm^3/40 cm = l + b

25 cm = l + b.

(40) (D) 600 cm^2.

Height of the cuboid = 20 cm

Perimeter of the cuboid's base = 30 cm

Lateral surface of the cuboid = perimeter of base * height

LSA = 30 cm * 20 cm = 600 cm^2.

(41) (C) 592 cm^2.

Length = 10 cm

Width = 8 cm

Height = 12 cm

TSA of a cuboid = 2 [(l * b) + (l * h) + (b * h)]

TSA = 2 [(10 cm * 8 cm) + (10 cm * 12 cm) + (8 cm * 12 cm) = 2 [(80 cm^2) + (120 cm^2) + (96 cm^2)]

TSA = 2 (296 cm^2) = 592 cm^2.

(42) (D) 600 cm^3.

Base area of cuboid = 20 cm

Base area of cuboid = 30 cm^2

Volume of a cuboid = area * height

Volume of the given cuboid = 30 cm^2 * 20 cm = 600 cm^3.

(43) (C) 20 cm.

Base area of the cuboid = 22.5 cm^2

Volume of the cuboid = 450 cm^3

Volume of a cuboid = base area * height

$450\ cm^3 = 22.5\ cm^2$ * height

Divide through by $22.5\ cm^2$.

$450\ cm^3/22.5\ cm^2 = (22.5\ cm^2 * height)/22.5\ cm^2$

20 cm = height.

(44) (B) $(d_1 * d_2)/2$

The area of the rhombus is $(d_1 * d_2)/2$, where d_1 and d_2 are the two diagonals of the rhombus, respectively.

(45) (B) $250\ cm^2$.

Base of cuboid = 25 cm

Height of cuboid = 10 cm

Area of rhombus = base * height

Area of the given rhombus = 10 cm * 25 cm = $250\ cm^2$.

(46) (A) 40 cm.

Area of the rhombus = $200\ cm^2$

Diagonal 1, d_1 = 10 cm

Diagonal 2, d_2 = x

Area of a rhombus with diagonals d_1 and d_2 = $(d_1 * d_2)/2$

$200\ cm^2 = (10\ cm * x)/2$

$200\ cm^2 = 5\ cmx$

Divide through by 5 cm.

$200\ cm^2/5\ cm = 5\ cmx/5\ cm$

$40\ cm = x$.

(47) (C) 4.8 cm.

Base of the rhombus = 25 cm

Area of the rhombus = 120 cm^2

Height of the rhombus = x

Area of a rhombus with height h and base is b = b * h

$120\ cm^2 = 25\ cm * h$

Divide through by 25 cm.

$120\ cm^2/25\ cm = (25\ cm * h)/25\ cm$

$4.8\ cm = h$.

(48) (A) 1.

The probability that an event will occur is represented by P (E), and the probability that the event will not occur is represented by P (E'). In a system, P (E) + P (E') = 1.

(49) (C) 1/5.

Number of red balls = 3

Number of yellow balls = 2

Number of blue balls = 5

Total number of balls in the basket = 10

The probability of picking a yellow ball = number of yellow balls/total number of possible outcomes = 2/10 = 1/5.

(50) (C) 1/3.

Number of black balls = 5

Number of yellow balls = 10

Total number of balls in the room = 15

The probability of picking a yellow ball = number of yellow balls/total number of possible outcomes = 5/15 = 1/3.

(51) (B) 3/5.

Probability that the event will occur P (E) = x

Probability that it will not occur P (E') = 3/5

Recall that P (E) + P (E') = 1.

Therefore, 3/5 + x = 1.

x = 1 – 2/5

x = 3/5.

(52) (B) 1/6.

Sample space = {1, 2, 3, 4, 5, 6}

Total number of outcomes = 6

Number of possible outcomes = 1

Probability of rolling 3 = Number of possible outcomes/total number of outcomes = 1/6.

(53) (B) 10.

Given: 7, 9 and 14

Total number = 3

Sum of numbers = 7 + 9 + 14 = 30

Mean value = Sum of numbers/total number

= 30/3 = 10.

(54) (D) 11.

3 + 10 + 7 + 4 + x = 35

24 + x = 35

Organize the like terms.

x = 35 – 24 = 11.

(55) (A) 36.

Number of players = 5

Total number of goals = 35 + 30 + 35 + 40 + 40 = 180 goals

Average goals = total number of goals/number of players

= 180 goals/5 = 36.

(56) (C) 7.

Given: 2, 3, 3, 4, 6, 7, 7, 7, 8, 9, 9, 1, 1

Reorganize the numbers: 1, 1, 2, 3, 3, 4, 6, 7, 7, 7, 9, 9

Find the number that appears most.

Reading Test 3: Answers & Explanations

(1) (C) Missing lunch breaks.

While a heavy workload may indicate that teaching is voluminous, missing lunch breaks indicates it is overwhelming.

(2) (A) Teaching materials designed to make teaching more effective.

Visual aids are designed primarily to ensure more effective teaching and easier learning.

(3) (C) A table of contents.

Visual aids include graphs, infographics and other materials a creative teacher may think of. However, they do not include a table of contents.

(4) (B) Teachers can learn how to use the tool easily.

A simple learning curve means *easy to learn*. Thus, teachers can learn to use the teaching tool with relative ease.

(5) (B) Teaglo.

Teaglo is a teachers-only social network platform. On the platform, teachers can interact with their colleagues around the globe and engage in activities that can enhance their skills.

(6) (C) Transferring files.

WeTransfer allows you to share large files by transferring them to your colleagues. This enables teachers to share resources among themselves.

(7) (C) It is your contribution to growing the teaching profession.

When you share tips, resources and ideas with your colleagues around the world, you are contributing toward developing the teaching profession.

(8) (A) Edmodo.

Edmodo is an educational network where teachers and students from different parts of the world can connect, share ideas and build great teacher/student relationships.

(9) (C) Recipient's email address.

Whenever you have a file to transfer, simply upload the file and enter the recipient's email address and you are ready to go.

(10) (A) WeTransfer.

WeTransfer allows you to share large files by transferring them to your colleagues. This enables you and your colleagues to share teaching ideas and resources.

(11) (B) By creating goal-oriented groups.

On Edmodo, users can create groups to collaborate with like-minded teachers and create educational materials for teaching purposes.

(12) (B) By using it to create personalized teaching for them.

Teachers can use Edmodo to measure their students' performance. When necessary, teachers can contact parents to enable them to create personalized learning experiences for students.

(13) (A) Teaglo.

Teachers who are looking for employment opportunities may be spotted by job recruiters who visit Teaglo.

(14) (B) Not compulsory.

Not mandated, as used in the passage, means *not compulsory*. Thus, it is not compulsory for WeTransfer users to create personal accounts on the platform.

(15) (B) Hobbies and certifications.

Aside from your educational qualifications, you should include other personal details, such as hobbies, certifications and more that will improve your chances of getting a job via the platform.

(16) (B) Exchange ideas.

Rub minds with, according to the context of the reading passage, means *to exchange ideas*. Thus, teachers can exchange ideas on the platform.

(17) (B) Feelings-based.

Intuitive means *feelings-based*. Hence, teachers can intuit—essentially, use what they know about their students based on their gut, their intuition, their feelings—what their students need most.

(18) (C) Busy.

Hectic means *busy*. Thus, after a busy day at work, teachers can have a well-deserved rest if they use the right teaching tools and techniques.

(19) (A) Contributions.

According to the passage, each member's input, which refers to contributions, will help improve the teaching profession.

(20) (B) Equipped with.

Armed with is an idiom that can be replaced with *equipped with*. It implies that a certificate and writing and reading skills are types of teaching tools.

(21) (B) Antonym context clue.

Using *seriously* and *nonchalant* in the same sentence denotes the idea of using the former to explain the latter. That is an example of an antonym context clue.

(22) (A) Their learning styles and attention spans.

When dealing with students from different backgrounds, you should consider their learning styles and attention spans.

(23) (B) It shows consideration for students' individual differences.

Patience shows consideration for students' diverse personalities and individual differences, especially when a teacher handles each student according to his or her limitations.

(24) (B) The ability to discern the best teaching technique.

Critical thinking is a must-have skill for identifying the best teaching technique.

(25) (A) It makes you an effective teacher.

With critical thinking, you will be able to strike a balance between your expectations and your students' performance. That will increase your effectiveness.

(26) (A) Verbal, written and body language.

The three communication styles are verbal, written and body language. A teacher should find the most effective communication style for each student.

(27) (C) Body language.

Body language includes the use of gestures and facial expressions. You should be able to convey meaningful thoughts to your students even without expressing them verbally or in writing.

(28) (B) Communication.

If your students always have difficulty making sense of your teaching, you should work on your communication skills.

(29) (A) Worthy of imitation.

Exemplary means *providing an example for people to copy*. It simply means *worthy of imitation.*

(30) (C) Imitate.

When you take a cue from someone, you are copying or imitating them. Thus, *take a cue from* means *imitate.*

(31) (B) It helps shape them into well-behaved students.

With your leadership skills, you will not struggle to shape your students' behavior, especially if you set a good example for them.

(32) (C) To ensure that everyone understands you.

When you reach every member of your class, all of your students understand you.

(33) (A) It will test your ability to deal with your students according to their attention spans.

You need patience to teach your students, especially when they have widely varying attention spans.

(34) (A) More than a certificate and ability to read and write is required to become an effective teacher.

According to the passage, *goes beyond* means that you cannot count only on your certificate and literacy skills for effective teaching.

(35) (A) Loss of interest in teaching.

A lack of patience may cost you interest in teaching. For instance, if your students have different assimilation rates, you may be held back by slow learners. If you are not patient with them, you may lose interest in your profession.

(36) (A) Temperament.

Temperament is a word that can substitute for *disposition*. Both words refer to an individual's character.

(37) (C) Critical thinking.

Your ability to think critically and assess your students will help you identify and adopt the best teaching techniques for them.

(38) (B) Almost three-quarters of the human body is composed of water.

Seventy percent of the human body is made up of water. Thus, water makes up about three-quarters of the body.

(39) (B) 8 cups.

As an adult, you need about eight cups of water daily, according to experts. It replaces water loss and keeps the body hydrated.

(40) (C) Dehydration.

Insufficient water in the body can trigger dehydration.

(41) (A) It will sap you of energy.

If your body does not have the required amount of water, you will not have the needed strength to carry out your day-to-day activities. That is an effect of dehydration.

(42) (C) Water.

Water should be your primary source of hydration. Processed fruit drinks cannot provide the body with enough water to function properly.

(43) (B) Before you are thirsty.

The best time to drink water is before you are thirsty. Once you are thirsty, you are already dehydrated.

(44) (B) Watermelons.

Watermelons are water-rich fruits that can boost your body's water levels and thus support hydration.

(45) (C) Sitting for too long at a time.

A sedentary lifestyle involves sitting for too long at a time. Many people, due to the nature of their jobs, sit at the computer or desk for long hours at a stretch.

(46) (C) Jogging.

Jogging is a simple exercise that can boost your physical fitness. Other exercises are biking and rope jumping.

(47) (C) They burn excess body fat and keep you healthy.

You must engage in simple workouts to burn excess fat.

(48) (C) Diabetes and heart disease.

Overweight and obese people are prone to health conditions such as heart disease, diabetes and others.

(49) (B) By making sure you walk some distance daily.

If you use public transportation, get off a few stops away from your office and walk the remaining distance. Repeat when returning home in the evening.

(50) (A) They are rich in vitamins.

Fruits and vegetables are rich in different classes of vitamins that play one role or another in boosting your fitness.

(51) (A) It boosts the body's immune system.

Vitamin C boosts the body's immunity against ailments and infections.

(52) (A) It supports weight loss.

Fiber helps fight weight gain and supports weight loss.

(53) (C) By creating walking opportunities for themselves throughout the day.

If you own a vehicle, park it several blocks from your office. Learn to use the stairs instead of the elevator, except when absolutely necessary.

(54) (C) Lower levels of physical fitness.

According to the passage, using the elevator does not promote physical fitness. That is why people are advised to use the stairs instead.

(55) (C) A list of things you want to do.

Your bucket list is a list of things you want to do. Thus, when you include physical fitness on your bucket list, you make it a must-achieve goal.

(56) (A) Physical activity promotes physical fitness.

It can be deduced from the passage that physical activity promotes physical fitness. This is in addition to eating a diet that supports weight loss and fitness.

Writing Test 3: Answers & Explanations

(1) (C) Interrogative and descriptive adjectives.

There are interrogative, demonstrative, indefinite, possessive and number adjectives. However, there are no descriptive adjectives.

(2) (A) Interrogation.

Interrogative adjectives are used for asking questions. *What, which* and *whose* are examples.

(3) (C) To describe nonspecific nouns.

Indefinite adjectives function as indefinite nouns. They describe nonspecific nouns. Some indefinite adjectives are *any, few* and *many*.

(4) (C) Number adjectives.

Number adjectives help readers find more information about the quantity of an object in a sentence. In this case, a number adjective would provide information about the number of boys in the vehicle.

(5) (A) What is he doing there?

This sentence contains the interrogative adjective *what*.

(6) (C) To join independent clauses to one another.

Adverbial conjunctions join independent clauses. They are otherwise known as conjunctive adverbs and include *however, in contrast* and *consequently*.

(7) (B) Helps find more information about the quantity of an object.

A number adjective helps readers find more information about the quantity of an object in a sentence. Thus, when looking for number adjectives, find an adjective that answers the question, “How many?”

(8) (C) They place an adverb after a verb in a sentence.

A common grammatical error that many make while using adverbs is that they place an adverb before a verb in a sentence.

(9) (A) He left home because he was late hurriedly.

“Hurriedly” is in the wrong place. It should not be at the end of the sentence. It should be after “home” or after “he.”

(10) (B) It is commonly used before the adjective or adverb it should modify.

Enough is an adverb that is commonly misapplied. The error occurs when this adverb is used before the adverb or adjective it is supposed to modify.

(11) (C) Noun-noun agreement error.

The girl and her twin sister are two people, or plural nouns. The referencing noun should be plural too. So it should be *dancers*, not *dancer*.

(12) (A) When two independent clauses are joined with a coordinating conjunction without a comma before the conjunction.

Coordinating conjunction errors occur when a comma is missing before the conjunction used to connect two independent clauses.

(13) (C) A correlative conjunction error.

If a writer mistakenly uses *or* for *neither* or *nor* for *either*, that is a correlative conjunction error.

(14) (A) Her boss complemented her for a job well done.

This is a typical example of frequently confused words. The appropriate word is *complimented*, not *complemented*. Although the words are homophones, they have different meanings.

(15) (D) The principal was unavoidably absent from the seminar.

This is the only error-free sentence in the list. The first sentence includes *assent* instead of *accent*. The second replaces *illusion* with *allusion*, while the third sentence should contain *effect* rather than *affect*.

(16) (B) Subject-verb agreement error.

The subject is singular. Thus, it must use a singular verb, or a verb with an *s*. The correct sentence is, "Olu loves going to the gym."

(17) (A) When a phrase or clause is not clearly or logically related to the words it modifies.

This error occurs when a clause or phrase is not logically or clearly related to the group of words it modifies.

(18) (D) Back.

Reversing back is redundant because when you put a vehicle in reverse, you are moving backward. Hence, the *back* in the expression is needless.

(19) (C) It has a parallel structure error.

The rule of parallelism stipulates that phrases or words in a series should maintain the same form. The right sentence is “He sings, dances and writes lyrics.”

(20) (C) Hitting your goals in life may be quite difficult, challenging and taxing too.

This sentence, unlike the others, does not have a parallel structure error.

(21) (B) By ensuring that the phrases or words you use in a series are of the same form.

When writing, consider the words or phrases you use in a sentence. They should be uniform to prevent a parallel structure error.

(22) (D) B and C.

Options B and C are correct. Option A contains *still yet*. That’s redundant. You should use either *still* or *yet* to avoid redundancy.

(23) (A) Forever and ever, close proximity and absolutely certain.

Examples of redundant words and phrases include *reverse back, plus in addition, past experience, absolutely certain, added bonus, at the present time, close proximity* and *forever and ever.*

(24) (B) She dance like a pop star.

This sentence is wrong because it has a subject-verb agreement error. The subject is singular, so the verb should be singular too.

(25) (C) By becoming familiar with such expressions and avoiding them while writing.

To prevent redundancy while writing, become familiar with such expressions and remember that redundant phrases or words are synonyms.

(26) (B) Pronoun-antecedent agreement error.

A pronoun-antecedent agreement error occurs when there is no agreement between a pronoun and its antecedent.

(27) (B) Identify the appropriate pronouns for each noun and use them accordingly.

You must use the appropriate pronoun when replacing a noun in a sentence to avoid a pronoun-antecedent error.

(28) (C) No error.

The sentence is correct. The *couple,* as used in the expression, requires a singular verb. Hence, *has* is accurate.

(29) (D) Subject-verb agreement error.

Subject-verb agreement errors are a common mistake many people make while writing. Writers often are confused about the most appropriate way to combine a subject and a verb in a sentence.

(30) (C) The cat and its kittens/loves.

This sentence violates the subject-verb agreement rule. *The cat and its kittens* require a plural verb.

(31) (A) A singular noun does not usually end with an *s,* while a plural noun does.

This is the distinction between a singular noun and a plural noun. Examples are *goat/goats, house/houses,* etc.

(32) (B) Both usually do not end with an *s*.

Neither a singular noun nor a plural verb end with an *s*. Examples of singular nouns are *book*, *pencil* and *chair*, while examples of plural verbs are *walk*, *go* and *sing*.

(33) (A) Does, goes, walks and sing.

This is the odd list out. While the first three verbs are singular verbs, the last verb, *sing*, is plural. Its singular form is "sings."

(34) (A) When it appears at the beginning of a sentence, begins a proper name or is used as a first-person pronoun.

Capitalize the letter *i* in the above situations.

(35) (A) When will the program begin, Senator?

Halloween should start with a capital letter, and the letter *I* should also be capitalized when used as a contraction. "Senator" is correct because when a title is used as a direct address, it should be capitalized.

(36) (B) To express strong emotions.

An exclamation mark is used to express strong emotions such as anger, happiness, love and hatred.

(37) (B) To indicate ownership and contraction.

An apostrophe is used to show possession or contraction.

(38) (C) I will visit my sisters' at work next week.

The apostrophe is misused in the sentence. Since the sentence does not portray ownership or possession, the apostrophe is incorrect.

(39) (C) Capitalization error.

When writing the titles of articles, books or works of art, capitalize the first letter of words. There are some exceptions, though. When writing these titles, do not capitalize conjunctions and short prepositions.

(40) (A) I will be available for the next tour of the Eiffel Tower.

Proper nouns should be capitalized. Examples are Federal Bureau of Investigation and names of people or places, such as the Eiffel Tower and New York City.

Essay 5 Answers & Explanations

(1) (C) Homicide.

Homicide is the number two cause of death of children between the ages of 10 and 19. It is the leading cause of death among Black males in the country.

(2) (C) Gun possession encourages crime.

It can be deduced from the passage that most gun-related crimes would not be possible if the perpetrators were not armed. Thus, gun possession encourages crime.

Essay 6 Answers & Explanations

(1) (D) LinkedIn.

LinkedIn is a social media platform where professionals and employers can connect to either look for job opportunities or hire qualified professionals. It is primarily designed for that purpose.

(2) (C) None of the above.

Social media offers job opportunities, provides learning resources and platforms, promotes social justice and helps people live their dream lives.

Conclusion

The Praxis Core test offers you the gateway to a dream career in the education sector. However, you must pass the test before you can live that dream. This guide helps you prepare for the examination and pass it.

Each section of the guide is tailored to address some areas the examination body will focus on during the test. Hence, it is beneficial to go through each section thoroughly and attempt the accompanying questions.

Learn as many phrasal verbs and idiomatic expressions as you can. Practice inference until you can draw logical conclusions from statements. Improve your ability to leverage context clues to glean the meanings of difficult words.

If you consistently incorporate the tips in this guide into your reading and preparation for the examination, you will stand a much higher chance at success.

Best of luck!

Made in the USA
Las Vegas, NV
15 August 2021